the great

prawn

and shrimp cookbook

whitecap

First published by: R&R Publications Marketing Pty. Ltd.

ACN 27 062 090 555

12 Edward Street, Brunswick Victoria 3056 Australia

E-mail: info@randrpublications.com.au, Website: www.randrpublications.com.au

©Richard Carroll

First edition published in 2004 in the US and Canada by Whitecap Books Ltd. This edition published April 2005.

For more information, contact Whitecap Books,

351 Lynn Avenue

North Vancouver

British Columbia, Canada V7J 2C4

Editor of North American version: Marial Shea

Publisher: Richard Carroll

Project Manager: Anthony Carroll

Food Photography: Andrew Elton, Warren Webb.

Food Stylists: Stephanie Souvlis, Di Kirby

Assisting Home Economist: Jenny Fanshaw

Recipe Development: Stephanie Souvlis, Jenny Fanshaw,

Ellen Argyriou, Di Kirby

Creative Director: Vincent Wee

Design: Icon Design

Proofreader: Andrea Tarttelin

National Library of Canada Cataloguing in Publication Data

Main entry under title:

The great prawn and shrimp cookbook / editor, Marial Shea ;

recipe development, Stephanie Souvlis ... [et al.]. –– North American ed.

(Great seafood series)

Includes index.

Previous ed. has title: The great prawn cookbook.

ISBN 1–55285–538–4

1. Cookery (Shrimp) I. Souvlis, Stephane. II. Shea, Marial. III. Series.

TX754.S58G73 2003   641.6'95   C2003–911237–3

Computer typeset in: Verdama, Trajan and Charcoal.

Printed in China by Max Production Printing Ltd.

The publisher acknowledges the financial support of the Government of

Canada through the Book Publishing Industry Development Program for our

publishing activities.

contents

Butterflying

This is usually done on green (uncooked) prawns. It is used to increase both the visual appeal and the size of the prawns.

Cut the peeled prawn lengthwise, almost right through the flesh and along its entire length. This can be done along the stomach, which is the traditional method.

Alternatively, you can cut along the back of the prawn to give a circular shape and larger appearance.

Shelling

1. Gently twist the head and pull it from the body.

2. Using your fingers, roll off the shell from the underside with the legs still attached to the shell.

3. Gently squeeze the tail and carefully remove the flesh. If you wish, the tail flap can remain attached to the body to enhance presentation.

Deveining

Using your fingers, strip the black intestinal tract (vein) out completely.

For uncooked prawns, you may need to use a small knife to make a shallow cut along the back before removing the intestinal tract.

SHRIMP OR PRAWN?

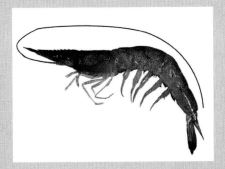  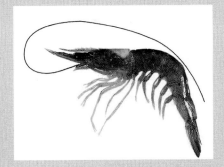

When is a shrimp a prawn? Is a prawn just a very large shrimp? This perennial question has no consistent answer.

Consult a scientific authority and you'll be told prawns are an entirely different species, related not to shrimp but to the lobster family, with miniature lobster-like bodies 6 to 8 inches long.

Sound confusing? That's because most of us are more familiar with the designation of prawns as large shrimp although, to add further confusion, even this is not consistent from region to region. In some areas, all shrimp, from small to large, are sold as shrimp (more technically correct). In other areas, only the small and medium crustaceans are called shrimp, while the large ones (15 or fewer to the pound) are called prawns.

In this cookbook, we are using this designation of prawns as any larger shrimp. Most of the recipes specify small, medium or large prawns. If you're still confused, the best thing is to find a knowledgeable local fishmonger. Describe what kind of dish you're preparing, and let your expert advise you about what prawns are freshest and most appropriate for your purpose. You'll soon be an expert in your own right!

TYPES OF PRAWNS

Tiger Prawns

As with all other prawns, there is virtually no oil in tiger prawns, and their moderate flavor makes them ideal for grilling, barbecuing, or flambéing.

Pan- and deep-frying are also popular ways of serving these prawns. Tiger prawns are large and flavorsome and their unique red striping makes for impressive presentation. They are popular served as garlic prawns and their flavor will be enhanced by marinating in olive oil, lemon juice and garlic.

King Prawns

These are probably the most sought after prawns, and as a result can command a relatively high price. They are extremely versatile and can be used for deep-frying, barbecuing, and pan-frying, and since their flavor is highly regarded, use of over powering marinades is not necessary. One drawback to king prawns is that poor handling and storage can quickly make the flesh go tough, so extra care is needed.

As well as different sizes, there are also many different types of prawns, from the succulent Tiger and King prawns to others that might be particular to your region. You may be lucky enough to have a supply of fresh ocean-caught prawns in your local fish shop. More commonly, you will have access to prawns that have been farmed and frozen, then thawed for sale. Again, don't be afraid to ask for advice. Your local fishmonger is one of your best resources for helping you shine in the kitchen.

APPROXIMATE COOKING TIMES

Cooking Method	Size	Time
Steaming	Medium – large size	10–15 minutes
	Small – medium size	5–10 minutes
Boiling and Simmering	Large size	5–6 minutes/lb (500g)
	Medium size	3–4 minutes/lb (500g)
	Small size	2–3 minutes/lb (500g)
Deep-frying	Medium size	2–4 minutes
Grilling (all types)	Medium size	2–4 minutes
Microwaving	Per $\frac{1}{4}$lb/125g in marinade	2 minutes

QUALITY ASSESSMENT

Test	Good Quality	Bad Quality
LOOK		
Shell condition	Clean, intact	Damaged, limp appearance
Color	Bright, glossy	Darkening around the edges of the body segments, legs, shell, flesh, or gut areas
		Dry, bleached areas
		Faded, discolored
Head	Firmly attached	Loose, discolored
FEEL		
Flesh	Firm	Soft, slimy, gritty
SMELL	Mild, very slight prawn odor, sea smell	Sweet "off" smell, developing to a strong prawn smell, chemical or ammonia smell

Note: Soft and broken shells may not be an indicator of poor eating quality. The shell may be soft because the prawn has just molted.

BUYING AND STORAGE

- Green (raw unshelled) prawns are available either whole or peeled and deveined, both fresh and frozen. Cooked prawns are available whole, shelled and deveined. For green prawns, look for a firm body with moist flesh and the shell to be tight and intact.

- Do not refreeze green prawns that have been frozen. If you plan to use prawns by the next day after purchase, all you need to do is remove from plastic bag, place in a bowl, cover lightly and place in the coolest part of the refrigerator. If, however, it will be a couple of days and you don't want to freeze them, the following are the best ways to store prawns.

- Green prawns — place in a bowl of ice water, refreshing with ice when it melts, and use within 2 days.

- Cooked prawns — place on a bowl of ice, refreshing when ice melts. Don't allow to sit in water as flavors will be leeched out. Use within 2 days.

- Leave all prawns in their shell. This protects them against dehydration.

- To freeze green prawns, place them in a plastic container covered with water; do not add salt. Cover and freeze. The water forms an ice block that protects the prawns from freezer burn. To thaw, place in the refrigerator for 24 hours. You can freeze for up to 3 months.

NUTRITIONAL INFORMATION

Nutritional Information (per 100g raw)

Calories	Protein (g)	Fat (g)	Cholesterol (mg)	Omega 3's (mg)
85	20.5	0.6	130	120

SOUPS

The variety of seafood soups is almost limitless, ranging from classic bisques to substantial bouillabaisses. As the cooking time is so quick, prawn and other seafood soups are among the fastest of all soups to prepare, making them ideal for last-minute entertaining.

San Franciscan Seafood Chowder in a Bread Cup

INGREDIENTS

8 smallish round loaves of bread
1/4cup/50mL/2oz butter
2 leeks, well washed & finely sliced
2 onions, finely chopped
4 cloves garlic, minced
2 carrots, peeled and chopped
1 parsnip, peeled and chopped
2 stalks celery, finely sliced
1 tablespoon/15mL fresh thyme leaves
1/3cup/75mL all-purpose flour
8 cups/2 litres fish stock
2 lb/1kg mixed seafood (including
   green prawns, mussels, clams, squid,
   white fish)
1 cup/250mL heavy or whipping cream
1/2 bunch parsley, chopped
salt and pepper (to taste)
juice of 1 large lemon
1/2 bunch of chives, chopped

METHOD

1. Preheat oven to 400°F/200°C. First, prepare the bread bowls. Using a sharp knife, cut a large hole in the top of the bread loaf, then remove this crusty top and set aside. Carefully remove all the soft bread from the inside of the loaf leaving the surrounding crust intact.

2. Place the loaves in the preheated oven and bake for 15 minutes until the loaves are crisp and dry. Set aside.

3. Melt the butter in a large saucepan and add the chopped leeks, onions, garlic, carrots, parsnip, celery and thyme leaves. Sauté in the butter for 10 minutes until the vegetables are soft and golden. Remove the pan from the heat and sprinkle the flour over the vegetables, stirring constantly to mix the flour with the butter. Return the pan to the heat and continue stirring until the mixture begins to turn golden (about 2 minutes). This gives the flour a cooked flavor.

4. Add the fish stock, stirring constantly to dissolve the roux mixture into the liquid, the simmer the soup for 20 minutes. Meanwhile, prepare the seafood by cutting the fish and shellfish into bite-sized pieces.

5. Add all the shellfish, cream, parsley and salt and pepper (to taste), and cook for a further 5 minutes. Do not allow the soup to boil rapidly because it may curdle. Once the shellfish has cooked, stir in the lemon juice and ladle the soup into the bread bowls. Garnish with a some chopped chives and serv

Serves 8

Hot and Sour Prawn Soup

INGREDIENTS

2lb/1kg medium uncooked prawns
1 tablespoon/15mL vegetable oil
8 slices fresh or bottled galangal or fresh
  ginger
8 kaffir lime leaves
2 stalks fresh lemongrass, bruised,
  (or 1 teaspoon/5mL dried lemongrass,
  soaked in hot water until soft)
2 fresh red chilies, halved and seeded
8 cups/2 litres water
3 tablespoons/45mL chopped cilantro leaves
1 fresh red chili, chopped
2 tablespoons/45mL lime juice
shredded kaffir lime leaves

METHOD

1. Shell prawns and devein. Reserve heads and shells. Heat oil in a large saucepan over a high heat, add prawn heads and shells and cook, stirring, for 5 minutes or until shells change color. Stir in galangal or ginger, lime leaves, lemongrass, halved chilies and water, cover and bring to simmering. Simmer, stirring occasionally, for 15 minutes.

2. Strain liquid into a clean saucepan and discard solids. Add prawns and cook for 2 minutes. Stir in cilantro, chopped chili and lime juice and cook for 1 minute or until prawns are tender.

3. Ladle soup into bowls and garnish with shredded lime leaves.

Serves 4

Prawn and Chicken Soup

INGREDIENTS

1 tablespoon/15mL vegetable oil
1 onion, diced
1 red bell pepper, diced
2 cloves garlic, crushed
1 teaspoon/5mL finely chopped fresh
  ginger
4 cups/1 litre chicken stock
4oz/125g boneless chicken thigh or
  breast, sliced
20 uncooked small prawns, shelled and
  deveined
4oz/125g rice noodles
4oz/125g canned bamboo shoots,
  drained and sliced
5 button mushrooms, thinly sliced
1/4 head of lettuce, shredded
2 green onions, thinly sliced
2 tablespoons/25mL finely chopped
  cilantro
1 1/2 tablespoons/20mL soy sauce
freshly ground black pepper

METHOD

1. Heat oil in a saucepan over a medium heat, add onion and red pepper and cook, stirring, for 5 minutes or until onion is soft. Add garlic and ginger and cook for 2 minutes longer.

2. Stir in stock and bring to the boil. Add chicken, prawns, noodles, bamboo shoots and mushrooms, reduce heat and simmer for 5 minutes or until noodles are tender.

3. Stir in lettuce, green onions, cilantro, soy sauce and black pepper to taste and serve immediately.

Serves 4

ot and Sour Prawn Soup

Prawn and Chicken Soup

A seafood bisque of prawns (shrimp), crab or oysters is a mainstay in Manhattan restaurants. Offer small crackers or wafer biscuits on the side.

Classic Shrimp Bisque

INGREDIENTS

$1/3$ cup/75mL/ butter
3 tablespoons/45mL finely chopped onion
1 stalk celery, finely chopped
1 tablespoon/15mL all-purpose flour
2lb/1kg cooked prawns (shrimp), shelled, deveined and chopped
$3^1/2$ cups/875mL warm milk
$1/2$ cup/125mL/4fl oz heavy or whipping cream
2 tablespoons/25mL sherry
salt
freshly ground black pepper
paprika
freshly grated nutmeg
3 tablespoons/45mL chopped fresh parsley or snipped chives

METHOD

1. Melt butter in a saucepan over low heat, add onion and celery, cover and cook for 5 minutes, taking care not to let vegetables brown.

2. Stir in flour and cook for 1 minute. Add prawns. Gradually stir in milk until blended. Bring to the boil, lower heat and cook, stirring, for 2 minutes or until soup thickens. Stir in cream and heat through without boiling.

3. Stir sherry into soup and season to taste with salt, black pepper, paprika and nutmeg. Garnish servings with parsley or chives.

Serves 4

Manhattan-Style Bisque

INGREDIENTS

11oz/315g cooked prawns, shelled and deveined
$1/2$ onion, diced
$1/2$ cup/125mL tomato paste (purée)
$2^1/2$ cups/625mL chicken stock
$1/3$ cup/85mL/3fl oz heavy or whipping cream
$1/4$ teaspoon/1mL paprika
freshly ground black pepper
1–2 tablespoons dry sherry

METHOD

1. Place prawns, onion and tomato paste (purée) in a food processor or blender and process to make a purée. With machine running, slowly add stock and process to combine.

2. Place prawn mixture in a saucepan and cook over a low heat, stirring frequently, for 10 minutes or until the mixture comes to the boil.

3. Stir in cream, paprika and black pepper to taste and cook for 2 minutes or until heated through. Stir in sherry and serve immediately.

Serves 6

Spanish Fish Soup with Saffron

INGREDIENTS

2 tablespoons/25mL olive oil

2 large carrots, finely chopped

3 leeks, finely sliced and well washed

1 red bell pepper, chopped

1 green bell pepper, chopped

1 tablespoon/15mL Spanish paprika

large pinch of saffron threads

2 cups/450mL/16fl oz white wine

3 cups/675mL/24fl oz fish stock

14oz/400g firm white fish fillets

14oz/400g prawns, shelled and deveined

14oz/400g baby calamari or squid

2 tablespoons/25mL chopped parsley

1 lemon, cut into wedges

METHOD

1. Heat the olive oil in a large saucepan and add the carrots, leeks and bell peppers and sauté until softened, (about 10 minutes) Add the paprika and saffron, continuing to cook for a few minutes more.

2. Add the wine and stock and bring the soup to the boil, simmering for 15 minutes. Add the diced fish, shelled prawns and squid and simmer for a further 5 minutes. Garnish with parsley and serve with lemon wedges.

Serves 6

Spicy Prawn Soup

INGREDIENTS

4 cups/1 litre/1³/₄ pt fish stock
2in/5cm piece fresh galangal, sliced
  or 8 pieces dried galangal
8 kaffir lime leaves
2 stalks fresh lemongrass, finely
  chopped or 1 teaspoon/5mL dried
  lemongrass, soaked in hot water until
  soft
2 tablespoons/25mL lime juice
2 tablespoons/25mL finely sliced lime
  rind
2 tablespoons/25mL Thai fish sauce
  (nam pla)
2 tablespoons/25mL Thai red curry
  paste
1 lb/500g uncooked large prawns,
  shelled and deveined, tails left intact
3 green onions, sliced diagonally
3 tablespoons/45mL chopped cilantro
1 small fresh red chili, sliced

METHOD

1. Place stock in large saucepan and bring
to the boil over a medium heat. Add
galangal, lime leaves, lemongrass, lime
juice, lime rind, fish sauce and curry paste
and simmer, stirring occasionally, for
10 minutes.

2. Add prawns and green onions and
simmer for 5 minutes longer or until prawns
are cooked.

3. Remove galangal and discard. Sprinkle
soup with cilantro and sliced chili and serve.

Serves 4

Chunky Corn and Prawn Gazpacho

INGREDIENTS

4 large Roma tomatoes, washed and
  halved
1 yellow bell pepper, seeded
  and quartered
$1/4$–$1/2$ teaspoon/1–2mL Tabasco
  sauce
1 teaspoon/5mL salt, or to taste
2 ears of corn
1 small leek, white parts only
1 clove garlic, peeled
1 small Spanish onion
1 tablespoon/15mL olive oil
2 teaspoons/10mL mild, sweet paprika
1 lb/500g shelled raw king prawns,
  tails on
juice of two limes
2 tablespoons/25mL chopped fresh
  parsley
handful fresh cilantro, chopped
lime wedges, to serve

METHOD

1. First, make the spicy sauce. Process the tomatoes in a food processor briefly then pour the mixture into a large bowl. Process the yellow bell pepper pieces until finely chopped and add these to the tomatoes. Add Tabasco sauce and salt to taste. Set aside in the fridge for an hour or up to 8 hours.

2. Using a sharp knife, cut the corn off the ears. Heat a heavy frypan over a high heat then add the corn and dry fry the corn until it is slightly charred and golden brown. Pour into a small bowl and set aside.

3. Wash the leek thoroughly then place the white parts only, the garlic and the Spanish onion in a food processor and chop finely. Alternatively, chop finely with a knife. To the frypan, add the oil and heat, then add the finely chopped leek, Spanish onion, garlic mixture and the paprika and sauté over a medium heat for 5 minutes until the vegetables have softened and begun to turn gold around the edges of the pan.

4. Move the onions to the side of the pan and add the peeled raw prawns. Allow the prawns to cook for a moment or two until they are orange in color underneath then turn them over and cook the other side.

5. Bring the onions in from the side of the pan and toss with the prawns. Add the prawn mixture to the chilled tomato mixture and toss thoroughly. Add half of the charred corn and the lime juice and parsley and mix well before returning to the fridge to chill.

6. To serve, divide the mixture between 6 martini glasses or wine goblets and top with chopped cilantro and remaining charred corn.

Serves 6

Chunky Corn and Prawn Gazpacho

Tom Yam Gong

INGREDIENTS

3 cups/675mL/24fl oz fish stock
1 tablespoon/15mL chopped fresh
  lemongrass or 1 teaspoon/5mL dried
  lemongrass
$1/2$ teaspoon/2mL finely grated lemon
  rind
2 tablespoons/25mL Thai fish sauce
8oz/225g button mushrooms, sliced
1lb/500g large uncooked prawns,
  shelled and deveined
$1/3$ cup/85mL/3fl oz heavy or whipping
  cream
4oz/115g bean sprouts
2 green onions, cut into $3/4$in/2cm
  lengths
1 teaspoon/5mL chili paste (sambal
  oelek)
$1/3$ cup/85mL/3fl oz lemon juice
3 tablespoons/45mL chopped fresh
  cilantro
freshly ground black pepper

METHOD

1. Place stock in a large saucepan and bring to the boil. Stir in lemongrass, lemon rind, fish sauce, mushrooms and prawns and cook for 3–4 minutes or until prawns change color.

2. Reduce heat to low, stir in cream and cook for 2–3 minutes or until heated through.

3. Remove pan from heat, add bean sprouts, green onions, chili paste (sambal oelek), lemon juice, cilantro and black pepper to taste. Serve immediately.

Serves 4

Bouillabaisse

INGREDIENTS

6¹/₂lb/3kg mixed fish and seafood,
  including firm white fish fillets, prawns,
  mussels, crab and calamari (squid) rings
¹/₄ cup/55mL/2fl oz olive oil
2 cloves garlic, crushed
2 large onions, chopped
2 leeks, sliced
2 x 14oz/398mL cans tomatoes,
  undrained and mashed
1 tablespoon/15mL chopped fresh thyme
  or 1 teaspoon/5mL dried thyme
2 tablespoons/25mL chopped fresh basil
  or 1¹/₂ teaspoons/7mL dried basil
2 tablespoons/25mL chopped fresh
  parsley
2 bay leaves
2 tablespoons/25mL finely grated orange
  rind
1 teaspoon/5mL saffron threads
1 cup/250mL/8fl oz dry white wine
1 cup/250mL/8fl oz fish stock
freshly ground black pepper

METHOD

1. Remove bones and skin from fish fillets
and cut into ³/₄in/2cm cubes. Peel and devein
prawns, leaving tails intact. Scrub and remove
beards from mussels. Cut crab into quarters.
Set aside.

2. Heat oil in a large saucepan over medium
heat, add garlic, onions and leeks and cook
for 5 minutes or until onions are golden. Add
tomatoes, thyme, basil, parsley, bay leaves,
orange rind, saffron, wine and stock and bring
to the boil. Reduce heat and simmer for
30 minutes.

3. Add fish fillets and crab and cook for 10
minutes, add remaining seafood and cook for
5 minutes longer or until fish and seafood are
cooked. Season to taste with black pepper.

Serves 6

Prawn and Crab Soup

INGREDIENTS

6 tomatoes, chopped

2 onions, chopped

1 tablespoon/15mL vegetable oil

4 cloves garlic, crushed

1 tablespoon/15mL oregano leaves

2 bunches cilantro

1 fish head, such snapper, perch, cod or haddock

10 cups/2^{1}/2 litres water

2 uncooked crabs, cleaned and cut into serving pieces

12 medium uncooked prawns, shelled and deveined

6^{1}/2oz/185g fish fillet, cut into chunks

METHOD

1. Place tomatoes and onions in a food processor or blender and process to make a purée.

2. Heat oil in a saucepan over medium heat, add garlic and cook, stirring, for 1 minute or until golden. Stir in tomato mixture, then add oregano leaves and cilantro, bring to simmering and simmer for 15 minutes. Add fish head and water and simmer 20 minutes. Strain stock and discard solids. Return stock to a clean saucepan.

3. Add crabs and prawns to stock, bring to simmering and simmer for 3 minutes. Add fish and simmer for 1–2 minutes or until all the seafood is cooked.

Serves 6

Prawn and Wonton Soup

INGREDIENTS

Pork Wontons

8oz/225g ground pork

1 egg, lightly beaten

2 green onions, chopped

1 fresh red chili, seeded and chopped

1 tablespoon/15mL soy sauce

1 tablespoon/15mL oyster sauce

24 spring roll or wonton wrappers, each 5in/12^{1}/2cm square

10 cups/2^{1}/2 litres chicken stock

1 carrot, cut into thin strips

1 stalk celery, cut into thin strips

^{1}/2 red bell pepper, cut into thin strips

24 large cooked prawns, shelled and deveined

METHOD

1. To make wontons, place pork, egg, greens onions, chili, soy sauce and oyster sauce in a bowl and mix to combine.

2. Place spoonfuls of mixture in the center of each spring roll or wonton wrapper, then draw the corners together and twist to form small bundles. Place wontons in a steamer set over a saucepan of boiling water and steam for 3—4 minutes or until wontons are cooked.

3. Place chicken stock in a saucepan and bring to the boil over a medium heat. Add carrot, celery and red bell pepper and simmer for 1 minute. Add prawns and cook for 1 minute longer.

4. To serve, place 3-4 wontons in each soup bowl and carefully ladle over soup. Serve immediately.

Serves 6–8

SALADS

As a main meal or starter, a prawn salad is always welcome. Whichever one of these recipes you choose, you can be sure it will not only taste good but will also be good for you.

Peach and Prawn Entrée Salad

INGREDIENTS

7oz/200g dried peaches
1 tablespoon/15mL lemon juice
2 teaspoons/10mL lemon zest, grated
2 teaspoons/10mL brown sugar
$^1/_2$ teaspoon/2mL salt
$^1/_2$ teaspoon/2mL freshly ground black pepper
$^1/_3$ cup/75mL/2$^1/_2$fl oz sherry vinegar
2 drops Tabasco sauce
2 teaspoons/10mL Dijon mustard
1 egg
$^2/_3$ cup/150mL/5$^1/_4$fl oz light olive oil
1lb/500g salad mix
12 king prawns, shelled and deveined

METHOD

1. Place dried peaches in a flat dish. Mix next 7 ingredients together and pour over the peaches. Allow to stand at room temperature for 30 minutes.

2. Remove peaches from vinegar mixture. Pour the vinegar mixture into a blender or food processor, add the mustard and egg, and process until smooth. With the motor running, add the oil in a thin, steady stream. Dressing will become creamy and thicken slightly.

3. Divide salad mix among 4 plates and place 2 peach halves on slope of salad and arrange 3 prawns on each plate. Spoon dressing over the salad and serve immediately.

Serves 4

2

Prawn and Avocado Salad

INGREDIENTS

1¹/2lb/750g cooked king prawns
1 avocado, sliced
1 grapefruit, segmented
<u>Dressing</u>
2 tablespoons/25mL mayonnaise
2 tablespoons/25mL sour cream
1 tablespoon/15mL yogurt
2 tablespoons/25mL chopped mint

METHOD

1. Shelled and devein prawns.

2. Arrange prawns, avocado and grapefruit on a serving plate. Drizzle with combined mayonnaise, sour cream, yogurt and mint.

Serves 4

Mediterranean Salad

INGREDIENTS

1 cup/250mL couscous
2 cups/500mL/16fl oz boiling water
1 tablespoon/15mL olive oil
1 tablespoon/15mL balsamic vinegar
freshly ground black pepper
1 cucumber, sliced
1 green bell pepper, chopped
3 plum (egg or Italian) tomatoes, chopped
12 sun-dried tomatoes, sliced
2oz/55g marinated artichokes, drained
 and sliced
2oz/55g pitted black olives, sliced
6¹/2oz/185g cooked prawns, shelled and
  deveined (optional)

4oz/115g feta cheese, cut into
 ³/4 in/2cm cubes
2 tablespoons/25mL chopped fresh basil
 (or 2 teaspoons/10mL dried basil)
2 teaspoons/10mL finely grated lime or
 lemon rind

METHOD

1. Place couscous in a bowl, pour over boiling water and toss with a fork until couscous absorbs all the liquid. Add oil, vinegar and black pepper to taste and toss to combine. Set aside.

2. Place cucumber, green bell pepper, fresh and dried tomatoes, artichokes, olives, prawns (if using), feta cheese, basil and lime or lemon rind in a salad bowl and toss to combine. Add couscous mixture and toss.

Serves 4

Mediterranean Salad

Tomato, Corn and Prawn Salad

INGREDIENTS

2 cups/500mL cooked corn kernels

1 onion, finely sliced

7oz/200g shelled, deveined cooked prawns,
   cut into $1/2$in/1cm lengths

2 tomatoes, chopped

4–6 green onions, chopped

1 red pepper, seeded and finely chopped

2 tablespoons/25mL red wine vinegar

2 tablespoons/25mL olive oil

1 clove garlic, crushed

1 tablespoon/15mL fresh lemon juice

METHOD

1. In a large bowl, combine the corn, onion, prawns, tomatoes, green onions and red pepper, mixing well.

2. Mix together the vinegar, oil, garlic and lemon juice and toss through salad.

Serves 4

Avocado Seafood Salad

INGREDIENTS

6 baby octopus
1 lb/500g prawns
3 ripe avocados
<u>Dressing</u>
$^1/_3$ cup/75mL/2$^1/_2$ fl oz olive oil
2 tablespoons/25mL lemon juice
1 hard boiled egg, finely chopped
1 tablespoon/15mL fresh oregano,
  chopped
2 cloves garlic, crushed

METHOD

1. Remove heads from octopus just below eye level. Wash well. Drop octopus into simmering water, cook until just opaque, drain, rinse under cold water. Cut octopus into bite-sized pieces. Combine with dressing. Marinate in refrigerator overnight.

2. Peel and devein prawns, stir into octopus. Halve avocados, remove seeds. Pile seafood on top of avocado halves, garnish with lemon and oregano.

Serves 6

Couscous Salad with Seafood and Fresh Mint

INGREDIENTS

1/2 cup/125mL/4fl oz olive oil

1/4cup/50mL/2fl oz fresh lemon juice

1 large clove garlic, minced

1 teaspoon/5mL celery seed

salt and pepper to taste

1/4 teaspoon/1mL turmeric

1/4 teaspoon/1mL cumin

1^3/4cups/425mL/14fl oz boiling vegetable stock

1 lb/500g green king prawns, shelled, tail
 left on

7oz/200g small calamari rings

1^3/4cups/425mL couscous

3 tomatoes, finely diced

2 stalks celery, finely sliced

6 green onions, chopped

20 fresh mint leaves, finely sliced

METHOD

1. Whisk together olive oil, lemon juice, garlic and celery seed until thick then season with salt and pepper. Set aside.

2. Add turmeric and cumin to the simmering stock and stir. Add the prawns and calamari and poach gently for 2 minutes or until the prawns are orange then remove from the stock.

3. Place the couscous in a large bowl then pour the remaining spiced stock over. Stir well and cover then allow to stand until water is absorbed, about 10 minutes.

4. Fluff up with a fork and add prawn and calamari mixture, diced tomatoes, celery, green onions and mint. Add dressing and mix well.

Serves 6

Sri Lankan Prawn Salad

INGREDIENTS

Dressing

2 tablespoons/25mL lemon juice

1 cup/250mL plain yogurt

1 teaspoon/5mL curry powder

2 tablespoons/25mL mayonnaise

2lb/1 kg large cooked prawns, shelled
 and deveined

1 grapefruit, segmented

1 orange, segmented

2 bananas, peeled and sliced

1 onion, sliced

6 spinach leaves, shredded

3 tablespoons/45mL cashews, chopped

METHOD

1. To make dressing, place lemon juice, yogurt, curry powder and mayonnaise in a bowl and mix to combine.

2. Place prawns, grapefruit, orange, bananas, onion and spinach in a salad bowl. Spoon dressing over salad and toss. Sprinkle over cashews. Cover and chill.

Serves 6

Couscous Salad with Seafood and Fresh Mint

Prawn, Avocado and Mango Salad

Prawn, Avocado and Mango Salad

INGREDIENTS

2 cooked medium prawns, peeled, tails
intact
medium mangoes, cut into thin strips
large avocado, flesh cut into thin strips
tablespoons/25mL finely grated lime rind
1/2 teaspoon/2mL fresh chili, finely chopped
1/4 teaspoon/1mL cracked black pepper
tablespoon/25mL freshly squeezed lemon
juice
tablespoons/45mL olive oil
bunch dill

METHOD

1. Decoratively arrange the prawns,
mango slices and avocado on a serving
plate.

2. Combine the lime rind, chili, pepper,
lemon juice and olive oil, mix well and
pour over salad. Garnish with sprigs of
fresh dill.

Serves 4

Prawn and Green Bean Salad with Dill Sauce

INGREDIENTS

lb/1^1/2kg uncooked prawns
3/4 cup/175mL green beans, topped and
tailed
stalks celery, thinly sliced
green onions, sliced
tablespoons/45mL chopped fresh parsley
lemon juice
hard-boiled eggs, roughly chopped
Dill Sauce
1/2 cup/125mL plain low fat yogurt
1/2 cup/125mL reduced fat mayonnaise
tablespoons/45mL chopped fresh dill
freshly squeezed juice of ^{1}/2 lemon
salt

METHOD

1. Bring a large saucepan of salted water to
the boil, add prawns, cook until prawns
change color (about 3 minutes). Drain and
rinse under cold running water. Peel and
devein prawns.

2. Plunge green beans in boiling water, allow
water to return to boil, drain beans
immediately. Refresh under cold running
water and drain thoroughly.

3. Combine beans, celery, prawns, green
onions and parsley in a salad bowl, sprinkle
with lemon juice, toss well to mix. Cover and
refrigerate until ready to serve.

4. To make Dill Sauce: Combine yogurt,
mayonnaise, dill and lemon juice in a small
bowl, whisk vigorously until well blended.
Season to taste with salt.

5. Serve salad cold or at room temperature
with sauce in a separate bowl. Add chopped
eggs to salad after the sauce is added.

Serves 4

Scallop and Prawn Salad

INGREDIENTS

**12 uncooked king prawns, shelled and
deveined**
1lb/500g scallops
2 large onions, sliced

<u>**Dressing**</u>
2 teaspoons/10mL finely chopped fresh dill
**2 teaspoons/10mL finely chopped fresh
parsley**
**2 teaspoons/10mL finely chopped fresh
chives**
1 clove garlic, crushed
1 tablespoon/15mL lime juice
$^1/_2$ cup/115mL red wine vinegar
4 tablespoons/60mL vegetable oil
freshly ground black pepper

METHOD

1. Heat up frypan and cook prawns, scallops,
and onions for 3–4 minutes. Allow to cool.

2. Combine all ingredients for dressing, and
mix well.

3. Place seafood and onions in a bowl and toss
in the dressing.

Serves 6

Prawn and Papaya Salad

INGREDIENTS

2 teaspoons/10mL vegetable oil

2 teaspoons/10mL chili paste (sambal oelek)

2 stalks fresh lemongrass, chopped, or
   1 teaspoon/5mL dried lemongrass, soaked in hot
   water until soft

2 tablespoons/25mL grated fresh ginger

1lb/500g medium uncooked prawns, shelled and
   deveined

$^1/_2$ Chinese cabbage, grated

4 red or golden shallots, chopped

1 papaya, peeled and sliced

2 cups/500mL watercress leaves

$^1/_3$ cup/75mL chopped roasted peanuts

1 cup/250mL cilantro

LIME AND COCONUT DRESSING

1 teaspoon/5mL brown sugar

3 tablespoons/45mL lime juice

2 tablespoons/25mL Thai fish sauce (nam pla)

1 tablespoon/15mL coconut vinegar

METHOD

1. Heat oil in a frying pan over high heat, add chili paste (sambal oelek), lemongrass and ginger and stir-fry for 1 minute. Add prawns and stir-fry for 2 minutes or until prawns change color and are cooked through. Set aside to cool.

2. Arrange cabbage, shallots, papaya, watercress, peanuts, cilantro and prawn mixture attractively on a serving platter.

3. To make dressing, place sugar, lime juice, fish sauce and vinegar in a bowl and mix to combine. Drizzle dressing over salad and serve.

Serves 4

Seafood Salad

INGREDIENTS

3/4lb/375g calamari (squid) rings
1 tablespoon/15mL olive oil
3/4lb/375g uncooked medium prawns,
  peeled and deveined
1 clove garlic, crushed
1 bunch/1 lb/500g spinach
1 red onion, sliced
1 red bell pepper, cut into strips
2 cups/500mL snow peas, trimmed
2 tablespoons/25mL fresh mint leaves
1/4 cup/50mL nuts, finely chopped
CHILI DRESSING
2 tablespoons/25mL sweet chili sauce
1 tablespoon/15mL soy sauce
1 tablespoon/15mL lime juice
1 tablespoon/15mL vegetable oil

METHOD

1. Place calamari (squid) on absorbent paper towel and pat dry.

2. Heat oil in a frying pan over medium heat, add prawns and garlic and stir-fry for 2 minutes. Add squid (calamari) and stir-fry for 2 minutes longer. Set aside to cool.

3. Arrange spinach leaves, onion, red pepper, snow peas, mint and nuts in a bowl or on a serving platter. Top with seafood mixture.

4. To make dressing, place chili sauce, soy sauce, lime juice and oil in a bowl and mix to combine. Spoon dressing over salad and chill.

Serving suggestion: This dish only requires fresh crusty bread or rolls.

Serves 4

Seafood and Vegetable Salad

INGREDIENTS

2 cups/500mL cooked long grain rice
8oz/225g cooked prawns, shelled and
  deveined
8oz/225g canned crabmeat, drained and
  flaked
4oz/115g boneless white fish fillet, thinly
  sliced (optional)
1 cup/250mL button mushrooms, sliced
6 green onions, sliced
1 carrot, thinly sliced
1/4 cup/50mL sliced green beans
1 egg omelet, thinly sliced

Rice Vinegar Dressing
1/2 cup/125mL/4fl oz rice vinegar
2 tablespoons/25mL mirin
1 tablespoon/15mL soy sauce
1 tablespoon/15mL sugar

METHOD

1. Place rice, prawns, crabmeat, fish (if using) mushrooms, green onions, carrot and beans in a large salad bowl and toss to combine. Prepare and slice egg omelet.

2. To make dressing, place rice vinegar, mirin, soy sauce and sugar in a bowl and whisk to combine. Drizzle dressing over salad, cover and refrigerate. Just prior to serving, top with omelet strips.

Serves 6

Seafood Salad

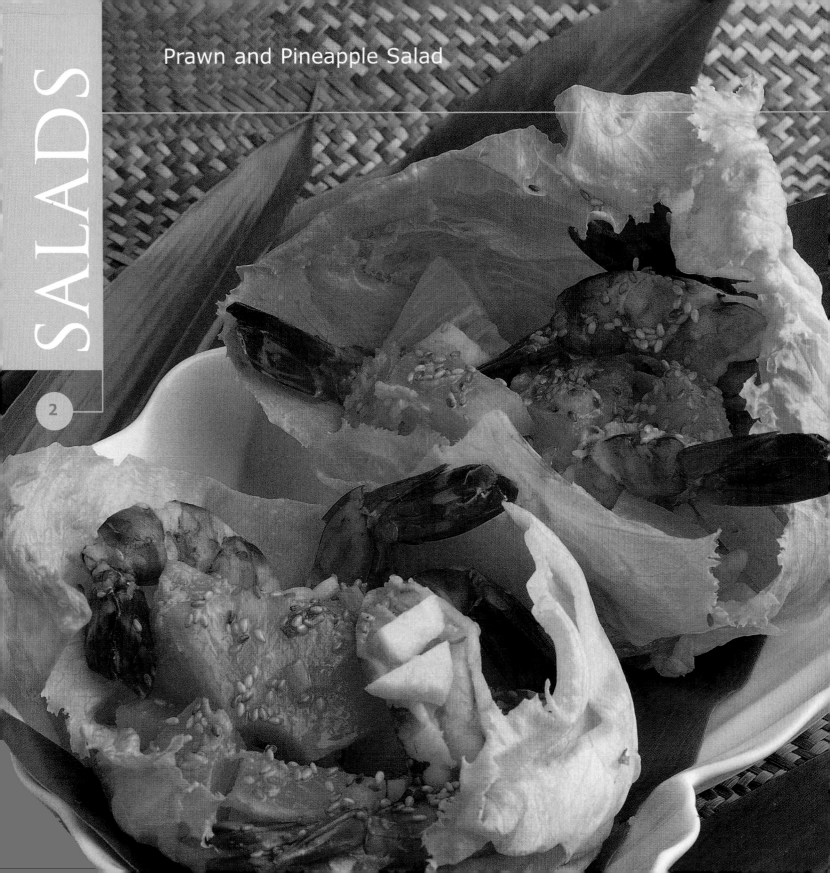

Prawn and Pineapple Salad

2

Prawn and Pineapple Salad

INGREDIENTS

1 tablespoon/15mL fresh lemon juice
2 tablespoons/25mL white wine vinegar
1 tablespoon/15mL Dijon mustard
1/4 cup/50mL/2fl oz olive oil
2 tablepoons/25mL Asian sesame oil
10 water chestnuts, drained and chopped
1 tablespoon/15mL grated green ginger
10oz/284mL can sliced pineapple, drained
   and cut into chunks
1lb/500g cooked prawns, shelled
lettuce for serving
3 green onions, sliced
1 tablespoon/15mL sesame seeds, toasted
   lightly

METHOD

1. To make dressing, whisk the lemon juice, vinegar and mustard together then gradually add the oils, whisking all the time until dressing is thickened.

2. In a bowl combine the chopped water chestnuts, ginger, pineapple and prawns. Add the dressing and toss together lightly.

3. Arrange the salad on lettuce cups and garnish with green onion and sesame seeds.

Serves 4

Prawn and White Bean Salad

INGREDIENTS

3 x 10oz/284mL cans cannellini beans,
   rinsed and drained
1 cup/250mL celery, thinly sliced
1 small red onion, thinly sliced
6 tablespoon olive oil
3 cloves garlic, chopped
1/2 teaspoon/2mL dried hot red
   pepper flakes
11/2lb/750g prawns, shelled and
   deveined
1/4 cup/50mL lemon juice, or to taste
3 tablespoons/45mL chopped fresh parsley
1 tablespoon/15mL finely chopped fresh
   oregano (or 1 teaspoon/5mL dried
   oregano
salt and black pepper to taste
8 lettuce leaves

METHOD

1. Place drained beans, celery and onion in a bowl and lightly mix to combine. Heat half the oil in a large heavy frying pan and cook garlic and red pepper flakes for 30 seconds or until fragrant. Add prawns and cook, stirring, for 2–3 minutes or until just tender.

2. Add prawn mixture to beans with lemon juice, remaining oil, herbs, salt and black pepper to taste and toss well. Cover and chill.

3. To serve, arrange 2 lettuce leaves on each plate and top with salad.

Serves 4

Prawn and Snow Pea Salad with Sweet Chili Sauce

INGREDIENTS

$3/4$ cup/175mL/6fl oz sweet white wine
1 tablespoon/15mL freshly squeezed lemon juice
1 tablespoon/15mL freshly squeezed lime juice
1 teaspoon/5mL sugar
1 teaspoon/5mL chili paste (sambal oelek)
1 teaspoon/5mL cracked black pepper
$1/2$ teaspoon/2mL ground coriander
$10^{1}/2$oz/300g scallops
$10^{1}/2$oz/300g green king prawns, shelled, deveined and tails intact
$3/4$ cup/150mL snow peas
2 tablespoons/25mL oil
1 tablespoon/15mL chopped parsley

METHOD

1. Heat the wine, lemon juice, lime juice, sugar, chili paste, pepper and coriander in a large frying pan over moderate heat until boiling.

2. Reduce heat, simmer, add scallops and prawns, cook for 2 minutes or until cooked through. Remove and set aside.

3. Add snow peas to the frying pan, cook for 30 seconds, remove with slotted spoon and add to the prawns and scallops.

4. Add the oil and parsley to the pan juices, cook for 1 minute, then pour over scallops, prawns and snow peas. Toss well and chill until ready to serve.

Serves 4

OUTDOOR PRAWNS

Whether it's a special celebration or just a few friends around for a bite to eat, barbecuing is a wonderful way to entertain. With their quick cooking times, prawns are perfect for barbecuing. This imaginative selection of dishes will have you serving these water creatures from the barbecue regularly.

Barbecued Marinated Prawns

INGREDIENTS

Chili and Herb Marinade
2 fresh red chilies, chopped
2 cloves garlic, crushed
1 tablespoon/15mL chopped fresh oregano
1 tablespoon/15mL chopped fresh parsley
1/4 cup/50mL/2fl oz olive oil
2 tablespoons/25mL balsamic vinegar
freshly ground black pepper
2lb/1kg uncooked medium prawns, shelled
  and deveined, tails left intact

METHOD

1. Preheat barbecue to medium heat.

2. To make marinade, place chilies, garlic, oregano, parsley, oil, vinegar and black pepper to taste in a bowl and mix to combine.

Add prawns, toss to coat and marinate for 10 minutes.

3. Drain prawns and cook on oiled barbecue for 1–2 minutes each side or until prawns just change color.
Serves 8

Hot Chili Prawns

INGREDIENTS

Chili Marinade
2 teaspoons/10mL cracked black pepper
2 tablespoons/25mL sweet chili sauce
1 tablespoon/15mL soy sauce
1 clove garlic, crushed
1/4 cup/50mL/2fl oz lemon juice

3lb/1¹/2 kg uncooked large prawns,
  peeled and deveined with tails left
  intact

Mango Cream
1 mango, peeled, pitted and roughly
  chopped
3 tablespoons/45mL coconut milk

METHOD

1. To make marinade, place black pepper, chili sauce, soy sauce, garlic and lemon juice in a bowl and mix to combine. Add prawns, toss to coat, cover and set aside to marinate for 1 hour. Toss several times during marinating.

2. To make Mango Cream, place mango flesh and coconut milk in a food processor or blender and process until smooth.

3. Preheat barbecue to a medium heat. Drain prawns and cook on lightly oiled barbecue for 3–4 minutes or until prawns change color. Serve immediately with Mango Cream.

Coconut milk: This can be purchased in a number of forms: canned, as a long-life product in cartons, or as a powder to which you add water. Once opened it has a short life and should be used within a day or so. It is available from Asian food stores and some supermarkets, however if you have trouble finding it you can easily make your own. To make coconut milk, place 1 lb/500g desiccated coconut in a bowl and add 3 cups/750mL of boiling water. Set aside to stand for 30 minutes, then strain, squeezing the coconut to extract as much liquid as possible. This will make a thick coconut milk. The coconut can be used again to make a weaker coconut milk.

Serves 6

Hot Chili Prawns

Seafood Paella

INGREDIENTS

1 tablespoon/15mL olive oil
2 onions, chopped
2 cloves garlic, crushed
1 tablespoon/15mL fresh thyme leaves
2 teaspoons/10mL finely grated lemon rind
4 ripe tomatoes, chopped
$2^1/2$ cups/625mL short-grain white rice
pinch saffron threads soaked in
  2 cups/500mL water
4 cups/1L chicken or fish stock
2 cups/500mL fresh or frozen peas
2 red bell peppers, chopped
2 lb/1kg mussels, scrubbed and
  beards removed
1 lb/500g firm white fish fillets, chopped
11oz/315g peeled uncooked prawns
7oz/200g scallops
3 squid (calamari) tubes, sliced
1 tablespoon/15mL chopped fresh parsley

METHOD

1. Preheat barbecue to a medium heat. Place a large paella or frying pan on barbecue, add oil and heat. Add onions, garlic, thyme leaves and lemon rind and cook for 3 minutes or until onion is soft.

2. Add tomatoes and cook, stirring, for 4 minutes. Add rice and cook, stirring, for 4 minutes longer or until rice is translucent. Stir in saffron mixture and stock and bring to simmering. Simmer, stirring occasionally, for 30 minutes or until rice has absorbed almost all of the liquid.

3. Stir in peas, red bell peppers and mussels and cook for 2 minutes. Add fish, prawns and scallops and cook, stirring, for 2–3 minutes. Stir in squid (calamari) and parsley and cook, stirring, for 1–2 minutes longer or until seafood is cooked.

Serves 8

Seafood Paella

Marinated Prawns Wrapped in Bacon

INGREDIENTS

32 green king prawns, peeled and deveined
$^1/_4$ cup/50mL/2fl oz fresh lime juice
1 clove garlic, crushed
1 tablespoon/15mL grated fresh ginger
2 tablespoons/25mL brown sugar
16 bacon strips, rind removed
16 wooden skewers

METHOD

1. Place prawns in a medium bowl with the lime juice, garlic, ginger and sugar and mix well. Cover and refrigerate for 30 minutes.

2. Cut bacon into strips about 1in/ 2$^1/_2$cm wide and wrap around each prawn. Thread two prawns onto each skewer.

3. Grill under a moderate heat for 2 minutes each side or until cooked through.

Serves 4

ADD AN EXOTIC TOUCH TO YOUR
NEXT BARBECUE WITH
THESE EASY TO PREPARE AND
TASTY KEBABS.

Scallop and Prawn Sticks

INGREDIENTS
6 uncooked king prawns, shelled and deveined
1 lb/500g scallops
1 large onion, cut into eighths
6 wooden skewers

<u>Marinade</u>
1 tablespoon/15mL olive oil
2 tablespoons/25mL white wine
2 teaspoons/10mL finely chopped fresh dill
2 teaspoons/10mL finely chopped fresh parsley
2 teaspoons/10mL finely chopped fresh chives
2 cloves garlic, crushed
2 teaspoons/10mL grated lime rind
2 tablespoons/25mL lime juice
freshly ground black pepper

METHOD
1. Thread prawns, scallops and onion pieces onto the wooden skewers.

2. To make marinade, combine oil, wine, dill, parsley, chives, garlic, lime rind and juice in a glass dish. Season to taste with pepper. Add skewered seafood and marinate for 1 hour.

3. Remove seafood from marinade and grill for 2–3 minutes each side, turning and brushing with marinade frequently.

Serves 6

Vietnamese Barbecued Prawns

INGREDIENTS
Nuoc Cham Sauce
2 garlic cloves, peeled
2 dried red chilies
5 teaspoons/25mL sugar
juice and pulp of 1/2 lime
4 tablespoons/60mL fish sauce
5 tablespoons/75mL water

1 lb/500g large green prawns
6oz/185g thin rice vermicelli
boiling water
2 teaspoons/10mL vegetable oil
6 green shallots, chopped
1/2 cup/125mL roasted peanuts
1/2 bunch cilantro, chopped

METHOD
1. To make sauce, pound garlic, chilies and sugar using a pestle and mortar. Add lime juice and pulp, then the fish sauce and water. Mix well to combine the ingredients.
2. Slit prawns down back, remove vein, wash and pat dry. Cook the prawns over charcoal for about 5 minutes, turning once.
3. Add rice vermicelli to boiling water and boil for 2 minutes, drain and rinse under col running water.
4. Heat oil in wok or frying pan, add green shallots and fry until softened. Arrange vermicelli on warmed serving plates, top wit prawns, then sprinkle with shallots and peanuts. Pour hot Nuoc Cham Sauce over top and sprinkle with chopped cilantro.

Serves 4

Sesame Barbecued Prawns

INGREDIENTS
2lb/1kg medium–large king prawns
1/4 cup/50mL/2fl oz olive oil
1/4 cup/50mL/2fl oz red wine
4 shallots, finely chopped
1 teaspoon/5mL grated lemon rind
1/2 teaspoon/2mL cracked black pepper
12 bamboo skewers (soaked in water for
** 30 minutes)**
3/4 cup/170mL toasted sesame seeds

METHOD
1. Peel and devein prawns (leaving the tails intact).

2. Combine oil, wine, shallots, lemon rind and pepper, mixing well.

3. Thread the prawns onto bamboo skewers (approximately 3 per skewer).

4. Place the skewers in a shallow dish and pour marinade over. Allow to marinate for at least 1 hour.

5. Roll the prawns in the toasted sesame seeds, pressing them on well. Refrigerate for 30 minutes before cooking.

6. Cook on the hotplate of a well-heated barbecue for 2 minutes each side.

7. Brush with marinade during cooking.

Serves 6–8

Skewered Prawns

INGREDIENTS

1 lb/500g green prawns

Marinade
1 small onion, finely chopped
2 cloves garlic, crushed
1 teaspoon/5mL fresh ginger, chopped
1/4 cup/50mL/2fl oz dry sherry
1/4 cup/50mL/2fl oz olive oil
salt and freshly ground black pepper
12 bamboo skewers (soaked in water for
  30 minutes)

METHOD

1. Wash prawns thoroughly. Do not remove shells.

2. Mix together ingredients to make marinade. Pour over prawns, and let stand for 1–2 hours in refrigerator.

3. Thread prawns onto skewers. Grill or barbecue for about 10 minutes (turning several times).

Serves 4

Barbecued Chili Prawns

INGREDIENTS

<u>Orange Marinade</u>
2 tablespoons/25mL mild chilli powder
2 tablespoons/25mL chopped fresh
  oregano
2 cloves garlic, crushed
2 teaspoons/10mL grated orange rind
2 teaspoons/10mL grated lime rind
1/4 cup/50mL/2fl oz orange juice
1/4 cup/50mL/2fl oz lime juice

1 kg/2 lb medium uncooked prawns,
  in their shells
1 small papaya, seeded and chopped
2 tablespoons/25mL chopped fresh mint
lime wedges
sliced chilies

METHOD

1. To make marinade, place chili powder, oregano, garlic, orange and lime rinds and orange and lime juices in a bowl and mix to combine. Add prawns, toss, cover and marinate in the refrigerator for 1 hour.

2. Drain prawns and cook on a preheated barbecue grill for 1 minute each side or until they change color.

3. Place papaya and mint in bowl and toss to combine. To serve, pile prawns onto serving plates, top with papaya mixture and accompany with lime wedges and sliced chilies.

Serves 4

Barbecued Chili Prawns

Prawn Satays

INGREDIENTS
**2 lb/1kg uncooked large prawns, shelled
and deveined, tails left intact
8 wooden skewers**

Satay Sauce
**2 teaspoons/10mL vegetable oil
1 onion, chopped
3 teaspoons/15mL ground cumin
1 cup/250mL crunchy peanut butter
1 cup/250mL/8fl oz chicken stock
3 tablespoons/45mL soy sauce**

METHOD
1. Thread prawns onto skewers.

2. To make sauce, heat oil in a saucepan, add onion and cumin and cook, stirring, for 3 minutes or until onion is soft.

3. Add peanut butter, stock and soy sauce and cook over a medium heat, stirring, for 5 minutes or until sauce boils and thickens.

4. Brush prawns with sauce and cook on a preheated barbecue grill for 2 minutes each side or until prawns change color and are cooked. To serve, drizzle with any remaining sauce.

Makes 8

Scallops and Prawns en Brochette

INGREDIENTS
**1lb/500g green prawns, peeled,
deveined, tail intact
14oz/400g scallops
9 wooden skewers
9 pickling onions
6 bacon strips
2 tablespoons/25mL olive oil
1/4 cup/50mL butter
2 tablespoons/25mL fresh dill, chopped
2 tablespoons/25mL parsely, chopped
2 green onions, finely chopped
2 cloves garlic, crushed
freshly ground black pepper
2 tablespoons/25mL lemon juice
2 teaspoons/10mL grated lemon rind**

METHOD
1. Parboil onions until almost tender, drain and rinse under cold water. Cut each bacon strip into 3, roll each section up.

2. Thread prawns, scallops and bacon onto skewers, finishing with an onion on the end of each one.

3. Combine oil, butter, dill, parsley, green onions, garlic, pepper, lemon rind and juice, add seafood skewers, stand at least 1 hour.

4. Remove skewers from marinade, cook on preheated barbecue grill until tender, brushing occasionally with marinade.

Makes 9

Scallops and Prawns en Brochette

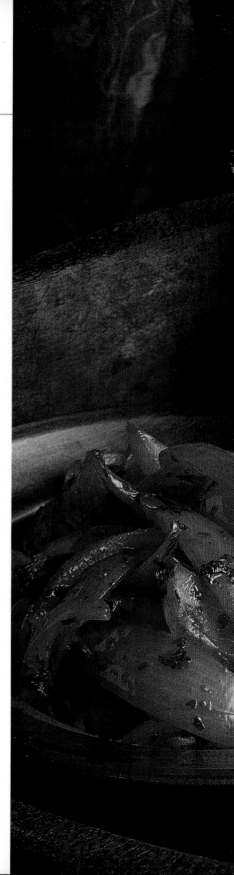

Chili Sesame Prawn Kebabs

INGREDIENTS

1 tablespoon/15mL vegetable oil

1 tablespoon/15mL Madras curry paste

2 tablespoons/25mL finely grated fresh ginger

2 cloves garlic, crushed

2 tablespoons/25mL lime juice

$^1/_2$ cup/115g/4oz plain yogurt

36 uncooked medium prawns, shelled and deveined, tails left intact

12 wooden skewers

6 tablespoons/90mL sesame seeds, toasted

Green Masala Onions

2 tablespoons/25mL ghee or butter

2 onions, cut into wedges

2 tablespoon/25mL green masala paste

METHOD

1. Place oil, curry paste, ginger, garlic, lime juice and yogurt in a bowl and mix to combine. Add prawns and toss to coat. Cover and marinate in the refrigerator for 2–3 hours.

2. Drain prawns and thread 3 prawns onto an oiled skewer. Repeat with remaining prawns to make twelve kebabs. Toss kebabs in sesame seeds and cook on a lightly oiled, preheated medium barbecue or under a grill for 3 minutes each side or until prawns are cooked.

3. To make masala onions, melt ghee or butter in a saucepan over medium heat, add onions and cook, stirring, for 5 minutes or until soft. Stir in masala paste and cook for 2 minutes longer or until heated through. Serve with prawns.

Serves 6

Chili Sesame Prawn Kebabs

Honey and Chili Prawns

INGREDIENTS

1/4 cup/50mL/2fl oz red wine
1/2 cup/125mL/4fl oz honey
1/4 teaspoon/1mL ground chili
1 teaspoon/5mL mustard powder
1lb/500g green king prawns
soaked bamboo skewers

METHOD

1. Mix all ingredients except prawns together to make marinade.

2. Shell the prawns, leaving on the tails, and devein. Place in a glass dish and add enough marinade to coat well. Cover and marinate in refrigerator for 1 hour. Thread the prawns onto skewers, either through the side or through the length.

3. Heat the barbecue to medium-high. Place a sheet of foil over the grill bars and place the prawns on the paper. Cook for 4–5 minutes each side: they will turn pink when cooked. Brush with marinade while cooking. Transfer to a platter. Remove skewers and serve immediately.

Serves 3–4

Teriyaki Prawns

INGREDIENTS
Teriyaki Marinade
1/2 cup/115mL/4fl oz soy sauce
2 tablespoons/25mL brown sugar
1/2 teaspoon/2mL ground ginger
2 tablespoons/25mL wine vinegar
1 clove garlic, crushed
2 tablespoons/25mL tomato sauce
bamboo skewers, soaked

2lb/1kg fresh green prawns in shell

METHOD
1. To make the marinade, mix all ingredients together and let stand for 1 hour for flavors to mix.

2. Shell the prawns, leaving the tails intact. Place in a non-metal dish and smother with the marinade. Cover and refrigerate for 1 or 2 hours. Thread onto soaked skewers. (For small prawns thread 2 or 3 per skewer. For king prawns thread only one from tail-end to top).

3. Heat the barbecue and place a square of foil on the grill bars. Place the prawns on the grill, brushing with marinade on both sides as they cook. Cook until prawns turn pink in color. Take care not to overcook.

Serves 4

Bacon and Prawns

INGREDIENTS

1 tablespoon/15mL Dijon mustard
1 clove garlic, crushed
$^1/_4$ red bell pepper, finely chopped
1 tablespoon/15mL finely chopped fresh dill
2 tablespoons/25mL olive oil
2 tablespoons/25mL lemon juice
freshly ground black pepper
12 large cooked prawns, shelled with tails
   left intact
4 strips lean bacon, cut into 12
   3in/7$^1/_2$cm strips
4 wooden skewers

METHOD

1. Place mustard, garlic, red bell pepper, dill,
oil, lemon juice and black pepper to taste in a
bowl and mix to combine. Add prawns and toss
to coat. Set aside to marinate for 30 minutes.

2. Preheat barbecue to a high heat. Drain
prawns and reserve marinade. Wrap a strip of
bacon around each prawn and thread onto
bamboo skewers. Brush with reserved marinade
and cook on lightly oiled barbecue, turning
several times, for 2–3 minutes or until bacon
is cooked and crisp.

Makes 4 kebabs

Avocado and Prawn Skewers

INGREDIENTS

2 avocados, cut into cubes
3 tablespoons/45mL lemon juice
20 cooked large prawns, shelled
10 cherry tomatoes, halved
10 bamboo skewers, lightly oiled

<u>Tomato Dipping Sauce</u>
$^1/_2$ cup/125mL sour cream
$^1/_2$ cup/125mL mayonnaise
2 tablespoons/25mL tomato sauce
2 teaspoons/10mL Worcestershire sauce

METHOD

1. Place avocado cubes in a bowl, pour
lemon juice over and toss to coat. Thread
2 prawns, 2 avocado cubes and 2 tomato
halves, alternately, onto bamboo skewers.

2. To make dipping sauce, place sour
cream, mayonnaise, tomato sauce and
Worcestershire sauce in a bowl and mix to
combine. Serve sauce with kebabs for
dipping.

Makes 10 kebabs

ASIAN
PRAWNS

Prawns and other seafood are extremely important and popular ingredients in Asian cuisine. The vast bounties of the sea are used in such varied and creative ways, it's little wonder why Asian-style cuisine is so appealing. Many of these dishes can be completed by plain rice or noodles of your choice.

Beef with Prawns and Noodles

INGREDIENTS

5¹/₂oz/155g rice noodles
1 tablespoon/15mL peanut oil
2 cloves garlic, crushed
8oz/250g lean ground beef
8oz/250g uncooked prawns, shelled
  and deveined
2 tablespoons/25mL sugar
2 tablespoons/25mL white vinegar
1 tablespoon/15mL fish sauce
1 fresh red chili, finely chopped
2 eggs, lightly beaten
1 cup/250mL bean sprouts
1 large carrot, grated
3 tablespoons/45mL chopped fresh cilantro
2 tablespoons/25mL chopped blanched
  almonds

METHOD

1. Place noodles in a bowl, pour over boiling water to cover and set aside to stand for 8 minutes. Drain well.

2. Heat oil and garlic in a wok or large frying pan over a high heat, add beef and stir-fry for 2–3 minutes or until meat is brown. Add prawns and stir-fry for 1 minute. Stir in sugar, vinegar, fish sauce, and chili and bring to boil, stirring constantly.

3. Add eggs to pan and cook, stirring, until set. Add bean sprouts, carrot and noodles and toss to combine. To serve, sprinkle with cilantro and almonds.

Serves 4

Chili Tempura

INGREDIENTS

Tempura Batter
³/₄ cup/175g self-rising flour
¹/₂ cup/125mL cornstarch
1 teaspoon/5mL chili powder
1 egg, lightly beaten
1 cup/250mL/8fl oz ice water
4 ice cubes

vegetable oil for deep-frying
1lb/500g uncooked large prawns, peeled
  and deveined, tails left intact
12 snow peas, trimmed
1 eggplant, cut into thin slices
1 small head broccoli, broken into
  small florets

METHOD

1. To make batter, place flour, cornstarch and chili powder in a bowl, mix to combine and make a well in the center. Whisk in egg and water and beat until smooth. Add ice cubes.

2. Heat oil in a deep saucepan until a cube bread dropped in browns in 50 seconds.

3. Dip prawns, snow peas, eggplant and broccoli florets in batter and deep-fry a few a time for 3–4 minutes or until golden and crisp. Serve immediately.

Serves 2

Serving suggestion: All that is needed to make this a complete meal is a variety of purchased dipping sauces, chutneys, relishes and a tossed green salad.

Chili Tempura

ASIAN

4

Coconut Prawns and Scallops

INGREDIENTS

2 lb/1kg large uncooked prawns, shelled and deveined, tails left intact
3 egg whites, lightly beaten
1 cup/250mL shredded coconut
vegetable oil for deep-frying
1 tablespoon/15mL peanut oil
4 fresh red chilies, seeded and sliced
2 small fresh green chilies, seeded and sliced
2 cloves garlic, crushed
1 tablespoon/15mL grated fresh ginger
3 kaffir lime leaves, finely shredded
$^3/_4$ lb/375g scallops
1$^1/_2$ cups/375mL snow pea leaves or sprouts
2 tablespoons/25mL palm or brown sugar
$^1/_4$ cup/50mL/2fl oz lime juice
2 tablespoons/25mL Thai fish sauce (nam pla)

METHOD

1. Dip prawns in egg whites, then roll in coconut to coat. Heat vegetable oil in a large saucepan until a cube of bread dropped in browns in 50 seconds and cook prawns, a few at a time, for 2–3 minutes or until golden and crisp. Drain on paper towels and keep warm.

2. Heat peanut oil in a wok over a high heat, add red and green chilies, garlic, ginger and lime leaves and stir-fry for 2–3 minutes or until fragrant.

3. Add scallops to wok and stir-fry for 3 minutes or until opaque. Add cooked prawns, snow pea leaves or sprouts, sugar, lime juice and fish sauce and stir-fry for 2 minutes or until heated.

Serves 6

Sour Prawn Curry

INGREDIENTS

19oz/540mL coconut milk

1 teaspoon/5mL shrimp paste

2 tablespoons/25mL Thai green curry paste

1 stalk fresh lemongrass, finely chopped
or $1/2$ teaspoon/5mL dried lemongrass,
soaked in hot water until soft

2 fresh green chilies, chopped

1 tablespoon/15mL ground cumin

1 tablespoon/15mL ground coriander

1lb/500g uncooked large prawns, shelled
and deveined

3 cucumbers, halved and sliced

$1/2$ cup/125mL canned bamboo shoots,
drained

1 tablespoon/15mL tamarind concentrate,
dissolved in 3 tablespoons/45mL hot water

METHOD

1. Place coconut milk, shrimp paste, curry paste, lemongrass, chilies, cumin and coriander in a wok and bring to simmering over a medium heat. Simmer, stirring occasionally, for 10 minutes.

2. Stir prawns, cucumbers, bamboo shoots and tamarind mixture into coconut milk mixture and cook, stirring occasionally, for 10 minutes or until prawns are cooked.

Serves 4

Stir-Fry Chili Prawns

INGREDIENTS
1 teaspoon/5mL vegetable oil
1 teaspoon/5mL sesame oil
3 cloves garlic, crushed
3 fresh red chilies, chopped
2lb/1kg uncooked medium
  prawns, shelled and deveined
1 tablespoon/15mL brown sugar
$^1/_3$ cup/75mL/3fl oz tomato
  juice
1 tablespoon/15mL soy sauce

METHOD
1. Heat vegetable and sesame oils
together in a wok over a medium
heat, add garlic and chilies and
stir-fry for 1 minute. Add prawns and
stir-fry for 2 minutes or until they
change color.

2. Stir in sugar, tomato juice and
soy sauce and stir-fry, for 3 minutes
or until sauce is heated through.

Serves 4

Spring Roll Baskets

INGREDIENTS

vegetable oil for deep-frying
8 spring roll or wonton wrappers, each
    5in/12cm square
2 tablespoons/25mL unsalted cashews,
    toasted and chopped

<u>Pork and Prawn Filling</u>

1 tablespoon/15mL peanut oil
2 teaspoons/10mL finely grated fresh
    ginger
1 small fresh red chili, finely chopped
4 green onions, finely chopped
8oz/250g lean ground pork
4oz/125g uncooked prawns, shelled and
    deveined
1 tablespoon/15mL soy sauce
2 teaspoons/10mL fish sauce
2 teaspoons/10mL honey
2 teaspoons/10mL lemon juice
1/4 cup/50mL bean sprouts
1 small carrot, cut into thin strips
1 tablespoon/15mL finely chopped cilantro

METHOD

1. Heat vegetable oil in a large
saucepan until a cube of bread dropped
in browns in 50 seconds. Place 2 spring
roll or wonton wrappers, diagonally, one
on top of the other, so that the corners
are not matching. Shape wrappers
around the base of a small ladle, lower
into hot oil and cook for 3–4 minutes.
During cooking keep wrappers
submerged in oil by pushing down with
the ladle to form a basket shape. Drain
on paper towlels. Repeat with remaining
wrappers to make four baskets.

2. To make filling, heat peanut oil in a
frying pan, add ginger, chilli and green
onions and stir-fry for 1 minute. Add
pork and stir-fry for 5 minutes or until
meat is brown. Add prawns, soy sauce,
fish sauce, honey, lemon juice, bean
sprouts, carrot and cilantro and stir-fry
for 4–5 minutes longer or until prawns
change color.

3. To serve, spoon filling into baskets
and sprinkle with cashews.

Serves 4

Thai Garlic Prawns

Thai Garlic Prawns

INGREDIENTS

cloves garlic, crushed
tablespoons/90mL cilantro
tablespoons/45mL vegetable oil
lb/500g uncooked large prawns, shelled
and deveined, tails left intact
4 cup/175mL water
4 cup/50mL/2fl oz fish sauce
tablespoon/15mL sugar
eshly ground black pepper

METHOD

. Place garlic, cilantro and
tablespoons/25mL oil in a food processor
r blender and process until smooth.

. Heat remaining oil in a large wok or
ying pan, add garlic mixture and stir-fry
or 2 minutes. Add prawns and stir-fry to
oat with garlic mixture. Stir in water, fish
auce, sugar and black pepper to taste
nd stir-fry until prawns are cooked.

erves 4

Gingered King Prawns

INGREDIENTS

in/5cm fresh ginger
large green shallots
2 cup/125mL/4fl oz peanut oil
2 teaspoon/2mL crushed dried chili
lack pepper to taste
tablespoon/15mL soy sauce
lb/1kg large green king prawns

Gingered King Prawns

METHOD

1. Peel the ginger and cut half of it into thin slices. Cut the other half into julienne strips. Cut the green shallots (half tops as well) into 2in/5cm lengths. Heat oil, add ginger slices, shallot and chili. Remove from heat, add black pepper and soy sauce and allow to infuse until completely cool.
2. Wash and then dry prawns and with small scissors, cut along top of shell and remove dark vein down the back. Leave shell and tail on and remove heads if you prefer. Toss the prawns in the cooled oil mixture and leave to marinate for several hours.
3. When ready to serve, heat grill until very hot and arrange the prawns on the grilling rack. Sprinkle with oil marinade and half ginger strips and cook until pink, then turn and repeat on other side.

Serves 4

Prawn Toasts

INGREDIENTS

1lb/500g peeled cooked prawns,
  deveined
6 green onions, chopped
2 teaspoons/10mL grated fresh ginger
2 teaspoons/10mL light soy sauce
$^1/_2$ teaspoon/2mL sesame oil
2 egg whites
6 slices white bread
$^1/_2$ cup/125mL fresh white breadcrumbs
oil for deep frying
cilantro for garnish (optional)

METHOD

1. Combine prawns, green onions, ginger, soy
sauce and sesame oil in a blender or food
processor. Blend until roughly chopped. Add egg
whites and blend until combined.

2. Remove crusts from bread slices, spread
them with prawn mixture, then cut each slice
into three strips.

3. Dip prawn-coated side of each bread strip
into breadcrumbs. Deep fry bread strips in hot
oil until light golden brown. Drain on paper
towels and serve at once, with a cilantro
garnish, if desired.

Makes 18

Prawns with Cilantro Butter

INGREDIENTS

$1^1/_2$lb/750g large king prawns, shelled,
  deveined, tail intact
$^1/_4$ cup/50mL/2fl oz olive oil
1 bunch cilantro
2 cloves garlic, crushed
salt, to taste
2 tablespoons/25mL lemon juice

Cilantro Butter

$^1/_4$ cup/50mL/2fl oz each of dry white
  wine and dry vermouth
1 tablespoon/15mL white wine vinegar
2 tablespoons/25mL green onions,
  chopped
$^1/_3$ cup/75mL butter
lemon juice, salt and pepper to taste

2 cups/500mL snow peas
$^1/_2$ red bell pepper, cut into thin strips
$1^1/_2$ cups/375mL Asian or button
  mushrooms

METHOD

1. Marinate prawns for a few hours in the
oil, half the cilantro sprigs, garlic, salt and
lemon juice.

2. Make the cilantro butter by combining
the wine, vermouth, vinegar and green
onions. Bring to the boil and reduce to about
3 tablespoons/45mL. Over low heat whisk in
butter in small pieces until the sauce
thickens. Season with a little lemon juice, salt
and pepper. Chop remaining cilantro and stir.

3. Heat a large frying pan and sauté the
prawns for about 2 minutes. At the same
time have a pan of boiling salted water
ready and drop in the snow peas, red bell
pepper and mushrooms for a minute.

4. Drain and toss the vegetables with the
prawns in the frying pan. Divide the prawns
on 4 plates, reheat the sauce and spoon
over each serving.

Serves 4

Prawns with
Cilantro Butter

Stir-Fried Tamarind Prawns

INGREDIENTS

2 tablespoons/25mL tamarind pulp
1/2 cup/125mL water
2 teaspoons/10mL vegetable oil
3 stalks fresh lemongrass, chopped (or
  2 teaspoons finely grated lemon rind)
2 fresh red chilies, chopped
1 lb/500g medium uncooked prawns,
  shelled and deveined, tails intact
2 green (unripe) mangoes, peeled and
  thinly sliced
3 tablespoons/45mL chopped fresh cilantro
2 tablespoons/25mL brown sugar
2 tablespoons/25mL lime juice

METHOD

1. Place tamarind pulp and water in a bowl and stand for 20 minutes. Strain, reserve liquid and set aside. Discard solids.

2. Heat oil in a wok or frying pan over a high heat, add lemongrass or rind and chilies and stir-fry for 1 minute. Add prawns and stir-fry for 2 minutes or until they change color.

3. Add mangoes, cilantro, sugar, lime juice and tamarind liquid and stir-fry for 5 minutes or until prawns are cooked.

Serves 4

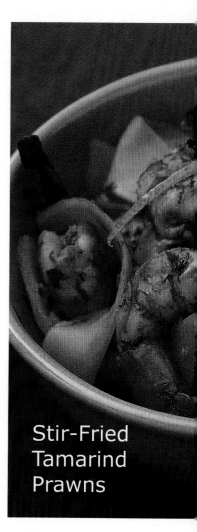

Stir-Fried
Tamarind
Prawns

Sesame Prawn Cakes

INGREDIENTS

11oz/315g uncooked, shelled and deveined
  prawns
8oz/250g fresh crabmeat
3 green onions, chopped
2 tablespoons/25mL finely chopped fresh basil
1 fresh red chili, finely chopped
1 teaspoon/5mL ground cumin
1 teaspoon/5mL paprika
1 egg white
3/4 cup/175mL sesame seeds
1 tablespoon/15mL vegetable oil

METHOD

1. Preheat barbecue to a medium heat. Place prawns, crabmeat, green onions, basil, chili, cumin, paprika and egg white into a food processor and process until well combined.

2. Take 4 tablespoons/60mL of mixture, shape into a pattie and roll in sesame seeds to coat. Repeat with remaining mixture to make six patties.

3. Heat oil on barbecue plate (griddle) for 2–3 minutes or until hot, add patties and cook for 10 minutes each side or until patties are golden and cooked.

Serves 6

Sesame Prawn Cakes

Lemongrass Prawns

INGREDIENTS

2 lb/1kg uncooked medium prawns
3 stalks fresh lemongrass, finely chopped
2 green onions, chopped
2 small fresh red chilies, finely chopped
2 cloves garlic, crushed
2 tablespoons/25mL finely grated fresh
ginger
1 teaspoon/5mL shrimp paste
1 tablespoon/15mL brown sugar
^{1}/2 cup/125mL/4^1/2fl oz coconut milk

METHOD

1. Wash prawns, leaving shells and heads intact, and place in a shallow glass or ceramic dish.

2. Place lemongrass, green onions, chilies, garlic, ginger and shrimp paste in a food processor or blender and process until smooth. Add sugar and coconut milk and process to combine. Spoon mixture over prawns, toss to combine, cover and marinate in the refrigerator for 3–4 hours.

3. Preheat barbecue to a high heat. Drain prawns, place on barbecue and cook, turning several times, for 5 minutes or until prawns change color. Serve immediately.

Serves 4

Fresh lemongrass and shrimp paste are available from Asian food shops and some supermarkets. Lemongrass can also be purchased dried; if using dried lemongrass, soak in hot water for 20 minutes or until soft before using. It is also available in bottles from supermarkets. Use this in the same way as you would fresh lemongrass.

Pad Thai

Pad Thai

INGREDIENTS

10oz/315g fresh or dried rice noodles
2 teaspoons/10mL vegetable oil
4 red or golden shallots, chopped
3 fresh red chilies, chopped
2 tablespoons/25mL grated fresh ginger
8oz/250g boneless chicken breast fillets,
  chopped
8oz/250g medium uncooked prawns,
  shelled and deveined
^{1}/3 cup/75mL roasted peanuts, chopped
1 tablespoon/15mL sugar
4 tablespoons/60mL lime juice
3 tablespoons/45mL fish sauce
2 tablespoons/25mL light soy sauce
4^1/2oz/125g tofu, chopped
^{1}/2 cup/125mL bean sprouts
4 tablespoons/60mL fresh cilantro
3 tablespoons/45mL fresh mint leaves
lime wedges to serve

METHOD

1. Place noodles in a bowl and pour over boiling water to cover. If using fresh noodles soak for 2 minutes; if using dried noodles soak for 5–6 minutes or until soft. Drain well and set aside.

2. Heat oil in a frying pan or wok over a high heat, add shallots, chilies and ginger and stir-fry for 1 minute. Add chicken and prawns and stir-fry for 4 minutes or until cooked.

3. Add noodles, peanuts, sugar, lime juice and fish and soy sauces and stir-fry for 4 minutes or until heated through. Stir in tofu, bean sprouts, cilantro and mint and cook for 1–2 minutes or until heated through. Serve with lime wedges.

Serves 4

Braised Prawns with Chinese Greens

INGREDIENTS

1^1/$_2$ lb/750g green prawns, shelled and
  deveined
1 tablespoon/15mL Chinese wine or dry
  sherry
1 teaspoon/5mL cornstarch
1 teaspoon/5mL soy sauce
12 snow peas
1^1/$_2$ cups/375mL Chinese flowering
  cabbage
5 tablespoons/75mL oil
<u>Seasoning</u>
^{1}/$_2$ teaspoon/2mL salt
^{1}/$_2$ teaspoon/2mL sugar
2 teaspoons/10mL soy sauce
1 teaspoon/5mL sesame oil

METHOD

1. Put prawns into bowl with wine or sherry,
cornstarch and soy sauce. Mix well, cover and
chill for at least 30 minutes.

2. Heat 4 tablespoons/60mL of the oil in a wok
and cook prawns until color changes. Remove.
Add rest of oil to wok and cook vegetables for
2 minutes.

3. Return prawns to wok and add seasoning.
Toss until heated through and serve
immediately.

Serves 4

Deep-Fried Chili Coconut Prawns

INGREDIENTS

3 eggs, lightly beaten
$1/2$ teaspoon/2mL chili powder
$1^1/2$ cups/375mL breadcrumbs, made from
 stale bread
$1^1/2$ cups/375mL shredded coconut
24 green prawns, shelled, deveined, tail intact
1 cup/250mL all-purpose flour
vegetable oil for deep-frying

METHOD

1. Combine eggs and chili powder in a shallow dish.
Combine breadcrumbs and coconut in a separate
shallow dish.

2. Roll prawns in flour to coat thickly. Dip in egg
mixture. Roll in breadcrumb mixture to coat.

3. Heat oil in a saucepan until a cube of bread
dropped in browns in 50 seconds. Deep-fry prawns in
batches for 2 minutes or until golden and crisp. Drain
on paper towels.

Serves 4

ASIAN

4

Singapore Noodles

INGREDIENTS

1lb/500g fresh egg noodles
2 teaspoons/10mL vegetable oil
2 eggs, lightly beaten
1 teaspoon/5mL sesame oil
1 onion, chopped
1 red bell pepper, chopped
2 cloves garlic, crushed
1 fresh red chili, chopped
8 uncooked large prawns, shelled and deveined
8oz/250g Chinese barbecued pork or
  Chinese roast pork, thinly sliced
6 green onions, sliced
2 tablespoons/25mL chopped cilantro
1 teaspoon/5mL sugar
1 teaspoon/5mL ground turmeric
$1/2$ teaspoon/2mL ground cumin
2 tablespoons/25mL soy sauce

METHOD

1. Place noodles in a bowl of boiling water and let stand for 5 minutes. Drain and set aside.

2. Heat vegetable oil in a wok over a medium heat, add eggs and swirl wok to coat base and sides. Cook for 2 minutes or until set. Remove omelet from wok, cool, then roll up and cut into thin strips.

3. Heat sesame oil in a clean wok over a high heat, add onion, red pepper, garlic and chili and stir-fry for 3 minutes. Add prawns and pork and stir-fry for 3 minutes longer.

4. Add noodles, egg strips, green onions, cilantro, sugar, turmeric, cumin and soy sauce to wok and stir-fry for 3 minutes or until heated through.

Serves 4

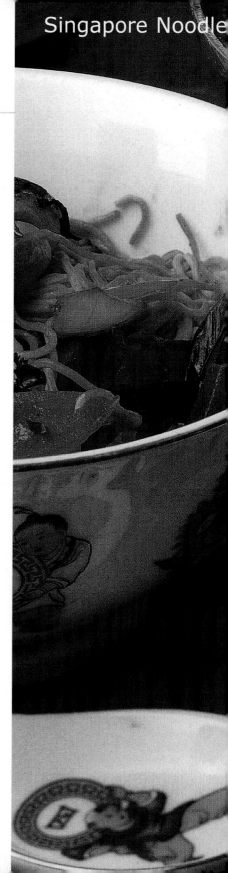

Tiger Prawns with Asian Dipping Sauce

INGREDIENTS

Dipping Sauce

1 clove garlic, crushed

$1/2$ teaspoon/2mL sugar

few drops of Tabasco

finely grated rind and juice of $1/2$ lime

3 tablespoons/45mL sunflower oil

salt and ground black pepper to taste

1 tablespoon/15mL sunflower oil

10 green tiger prawns, shelled, deveined, tails intact

4 romaine lettuce leaves

chopped cilantro to garnish

METHOD

1. To make the dipping sauce, mix together all ingredients.

2. Heat oil in a frying pan, then fry prawns for 3–4 minutes or until pink and cooked through.

3. Arrange lettuce leaves on 2 serving plates, scatter prawns over and garnish with cilantro. Serve with dipping sauce.

Serves 2

Tiger Prawn, Snow Pea and Mango Stir-Fry

INGREDIENTS

2 tablespoons/25mL vegetable oil

$1^1/2$ tablespoons/20mL grated fresh ginger

14oz/400g green tiger prawns, shelled, deveined, tails intact

$2^1/4$ cups/550mL snow peas

bunch green onions, sliced

1 large mango, peeled and thinly sliced

2 tablespoons/25mL light soy sauce

METHOD

1. Heat the oil in a wok, add ginger and prawns and stir-fry for 2 minutes or until the prawns are just turning pink.

2. Add the snow peas and green onions and stir-fry for a further minute to soften slightly. Stir in the mango and soy sauce and stir-fry for 1 minute to heat through.

Serves 2

Southeast Asian
Pan-Fried Prawns

INGREDIENTS

small red chilies, deseeded and chopped

cloves garlic, chopped

in/2¹/2cm piece fresh ginger, chopped

shallot, chopped

tablespoons/25mL vegetable oil

onion, chopped

lb/500g green prawns, shelled, deveined, tails intact

tomatoes, quartered

teaspoon/5mL sugar

alt

METHOD

1. Blend the chilies, garlic, ginger and shallot to a paste in a food processor or with a pestle and mortar. Heat the oil in a large, heavy-based frying pan or wok over a high heat, then fry the onion for 2 minutes to soften slightly. Add the paste and stir-fry for 1 minute to release the flavor.

2. Add the prawns and tomatoes, mixing thoroughly, then sprinkle over the sugar and salt to taste. Fry for 3–5 minutes, until the prawns turn pink and are cooked through, stirring often.

Serves 4

Fried Rice with Prawns

INGREDIENTS

/4 cup/175mL long-grain rice

/2 teaspoon/5mL salt

/2 cup/125mL frozen peas

tablespoons/25mL vegetable oil

cloves garlic, peeled and chopped roughly

green onions, thinly sliced

egg, beaten

1/2oz/100g cooked, peeled prawns

alt to taste

METHOD

1. Rinse the rice in a sieve. Bring a large saucepan of water to the boil, then add the rice and salt. Simmer for 10 minutes or until the rice is tender, then drain thoroughly. Meanwhile, bring a small pan of water to the boil, add the peas and cook for 3–4 minutes, until softened.

2. Heat a wok or a large heavy-based frying pan over a medium heat. Add the oil and rotate the wok or pan for 1 minute to coat the base and lower sides.

3. Add the garlic and green onions and fry, stirring constantly with a wooden spoon, for 30 seconds. Then add the beaten egg and stir briskly for 30 seconds or until it scrambles.

4. Add the cooked rice, peas and prawns and stir over the heat for 3 minutes or until everything is heated through and mixed in with the egg and green onions. Season with a pinch of salt.

Serves 2

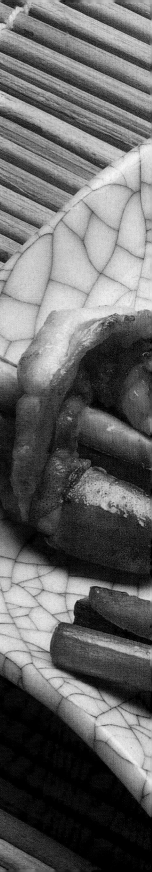

Butterflied Prawns

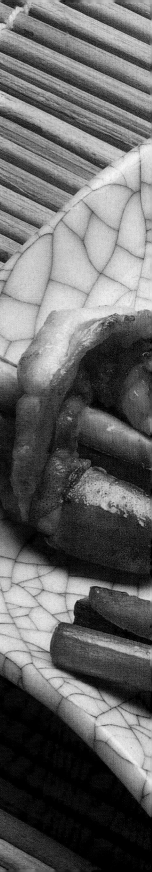

INGREDIENTS

1 lb/500g green king prawns
1 ham steak
1 zucchini
6 shallots
2 tablespoons/25mL vegetable oil

Dipping Sauce
2 tablespoons/25mL cornstarch, blended
  with $1/4$ cup/50mL/2fl oz water
1 cup/250mL/8fl oz water
1 chicken stock cube
2 tablespoons/25mL sherry
2 tablespoons/25mL soy sauce
2 tablespoons/25mL grated fresh ginger
1 clove garlic, crushed

METHOD

1. Shell and devein prawns, leaving tails intact. Make a shallow cut along back of prawn. Cut a $1/2$in/1cm slit right through the center of each prawn.

2. Cut ham, zucchini and shallots into thin straws, 2in/5cm long. Push a piece of each through the slits in the prawns.

3. Heat vegetable oil in wok or frying pan, add prawns and stir fry for 1 minute.

4. Combine blended cornstarch, water, stock cube, sherry, soy sauce, ginger and garlic, stir over heat until mixture boils and thickens; use as a dipping sauce for prawns.

Makes 24

ASIAN

4

Vietnamese Crêpes with a Dipping Sauce

INGREDIENTS

Crêpes

250g/8oz rice flour

1 teaspoon/5mL salt

1^1/$_2$ teaspoons/7mL sugar

1 cup/250mL/8fl oz coconut milk (canned)

1 cup/250mL/8fl oz water

^{1}/$_2$ teaspoon/2mL ground turmeric

7oz/200g shelled king prawns

7oz/200g bean shoots

3^1/$_2$ oz/100g pork or chicken fillet

1 onion, sliced

peanut oil (for frying)

Dipping Sauce

3 teaspoons/15mL fish sauce

5 teaspoons/25mL sugar

2 tablespoons/25mL water

1 tiny red chili (minced)

1 clove garlic (minced)

Vietnamese mint leaves (for serving)

iceberg lettuce leaves (for serving)

METHOD

1. First, make the batter. Mix together the rice flour, salt, sugar, coconut milk, water and turmeric until the batter is smooth.

2. Wash and dry the prawns and chop roughly. Wash the bean shoots, dice the pork or chicken, slice the onions and set aside.

3. Heat a large frying pan and pour in a little oil. Add the pork or chicken, onion and prawns, and cook, stirring constantly, until the prawns change color and the pork is cooked through.

4. Pour enough batter over the mixture to cover the ingredients, top with some bean shoots and cover with a lid. Cook for 2 minutes until crisp. Turn over and cook the other side until golden.

5. Make the dipping sauce by mixing all the ingredients together, stirring well.

6. To serve, place a Vietnamese mint leaf on a piece of the crêpe. Enclose in a lettuce leaf and drizzle some dressing over. Eat immediately.

Variation: To make a vegetarian crêpe, replace the pork and prawns with 1 medium carrot and half a medium-sized red bell pepper (both julienned finely) and proceed as above.

Vietnamese Crêpe

Tuna and Prawn Sushi

INGREDIENTS

Sushi Rice

2 cups/500mL short-grain rice

2^1/2 cups/625mL water

2 tablespoons/25mL sweet sake or sherry

4 tablespoons/60mL rice vinegar

2 tablespoons/25mL sugar

^{1}/2 teaspoon/2mL salt

12 large cooked prawns, shelled, deveined, tails left intact

2 teaspoons/10mL wasabi powder

4oz/125g sashimi (fresh) tuna

1 sheet nori (seaweed), cut into strips (optional)

soy sauce

METHOD

1. For the rice, wash rice several times in cold water and set aside to drain for 30 minutes. Place rice and water in a large saucepan and bring to the boil, cover and cook, without stirring, over a low heat for 15 minutes. Remove pan from heat and set aside for 10 minutes.

2. Place sake or sherry, vinegar, sugar and salt in a small saucepan and bring to the boil. Remove pan from heat and set aside to cool.

3. Turn rice out into a large shallow dish, pour vinegar mixture over and toss gently until rice has cooled to room temperature. Take a spoonful of rice in your hand and gently squeeze it to form a neat oval. Place on a serving platter and repeat with remaining rice to make 24 ovals.

4. Split prawns on the underside — taking care not to cut all the way through — and flatten them out. Mix wasabi powder with a few drops of water to make a smooth paste and dab a little on each rice oval. Top twelve rice ovals with prawns.

5. Cut tuna into twelve ^{3}/4 x 1^1/2in/2 x 4cm strips each ^{1}/4 in/5mm thick. Top remaining rice ovals with tuna strips. Wrap a strip of nori (seaweed), if using, around each sushi. Serve sushi with soy sauce for dipping.

Makes 24

...ith a Dipping Sauce

Sesame Coconut King Prawns with Mango Salsa

INGREDIENTS

12 raw king prawns, peeled, tail left on
salt and pepper to taste
flour for dusting
1 egg, beaten
1 cup/125g/4^1/$_2$oz sesame seeds
1 cup/90g/3oz coconut threads
1 mango, peeled and finely diced
^{1}/$_2$ small Spanish onion, finely diced
2 tablespoons/25mL cilantro, chopped
juice of 1 lime
2 tablespoons/25mL butter or olive oil
assorted greens of your choice

METHOD

1. Butterfly the prawns (see page 4) then dust
with salt, pepper and flour. Dip in egg, allowing
the excess to run off, then dredge in a mixture
of sesame seeds and coconut. Set aside.

2. Mix the mango, onion, cilantro and lime juice
in a bowl and season to taste.

3. Heat the butter or olive oil in a frypan, add
the king prawns and fry over a high heat for
1–2 minutes each side until golden.

4. To serve, arrange some greens on each plate
and top with 3 cooked prawns and a generous
spoonful of the mango salsa.

Serves 4

Honeyed Prawn Chow Mein

INGREDIENTS

2 tablespoons/25mL vegetable oil
1 clove garlic, crushed
1 onion, chopped
2 stalks celery, sliced
1^1/$_2$ cups/375mL button mushrooms, sliced
^{1}/$_2$ cup/125mL snow peas
114mL/4oz canned bamboo shoots, drained
114mL/4oz canned water chestnuts,
  drained and sliced
1^1/$_2$lb/750g large uncooked prawns,
  shelled and deveined, with tails intact
^{1}/$_4$ cup/50mL honey
1 tablespoon/15mL dry sherry
1 tablespoon/15mL soy sauce
1 tablespoon/15mL sesame seeds, toasted

METHOD

1. Heat oil in a wok or frying pan over a
medium heat, add garlic and stir-fry for
30 seconds. Add onion and celery and stir-
fry for 1 minute. Add mushrooms, snow
peas, bamboo shoots and water chestnuts
and stir-fry for 3 minutes longer or until
vegetables are just tender.

2. Add prawns and stir-fry for 2 minutes
or until prawns just change color. Add
honey, sherry and soy sauce and stir-fry
for 2 minutes longer or until mixture is
heated through. Sprinkle with sesame
seeds and serve immediately.

Serves 4

Sesame Coconut King Prawns with Mango Salsa

ASIAN

Steamed Prawns with Ginger and Soy Sauce

INGREDIENTS

1 bunch cilantro

2in/5cm piece fresh ginger

2 tablespoons/25mL each sesame and vegetable oil

2 tablespoons/25mL finely sliced green onions

$^{1}/_{2}$ cup/125mL light soy sauce

2lb/1kg small–medium green prawns

METHOD

1. Wash cilantro and cut roots and stems off, chopping roughly. Reserve the leaves. Pour water into a pan to a depth of about 1in/2$^{1}/_{2}$cm and add the chopped cilantro stems.

2. To make sauce, peel and shred the ginger into very fine slivers. Heat oils almost to smoking point, remove from heat and add ginger and green onions. Leave to cool 15 minutes and stir in soy sauce.

3. Line one large or several small steamer baskets with cilantro leaves and place the prawns in one layer on top. Season with a little salt and cover with more cilantro. Steam over the cilantro water with the lid on for 5 minutes or until prawns have all turned pink.

4. Remove from heat and transfer to a serving platter. Serve with the ginger and soy sauce.

Serves 4

Nasi Goreng

INGREDIENTS

<u>Chinese Omelet</u>
2 eggs
2 teaspoons/10mL water
freshly ground black pepper

1/4 cup/50mL/2fl oz vegetable oil
1 onion, sliced
3 green onions, chopped
8oz/250g diced pork
4oz/125g shelled uncooked prawns
4 cups/1 litre cooked rice or
  2 cups/500mL raw rice, cooked
1 red bell pepper, chopped

3 tablespoons/45mL or other raisins
1/3 cup/75mL cashews or peanuts
1 teaspoon/5mL chopped fresh red chili
2 tablespoons/25mL soy sauce

METHOD

1. To make omelet, place eggs, water and black pepper to taste in a bowl and whisk to combine. Heat a lightly greased wok or frying pan over a medium heat, add half the egg mixture and tilt pan to thinly coat base. Cook for 1–2 minutes or until underside is set, flip and cook for 10 seconds. Remove and set aside to cool. Use remaining egg mixture to make a second omelet. Stack omelets, roll up and cut into fine shreds. Set aside.

2. Heat half the oil in a wok or large frying pan over a medium heat, add onion and green onions and stir-fry for 3–4 minutes or until onion is tender. Add pork and stir-fry for 2–3 minutes. Add prawns and stir-fry for 1–2 minutes longer or until prawns change color. Remove mixture from pan and set aside.

3. Heat remaining oil in same pan, add rice, red pepper, raisins, cashews or peanuts, if using, chili and soy sauce and stir-fry for 2 minutes. Return pork mixture to pan and stir-fry for 1 minute or until heated through. Top with omelet strips and serve immediately.

Serves 4

MEDITERRANEAN
PRAWNS

The lands lapping the Mediterranean—among them France, Italy, Greece and Spain—each have a unique culinary style. The Spanish have perfected paella, the French bouillabaisse, while Italians are famous for their pastas and the Greeks for their use of herbs, lemon and cheeses. Enjoy our selection of prawn dishes inspired by these classic cuisines.

Prawns with Sauce Verte

INGREDIENTS

3/4 cup/175mL dry vermouth
2–6 green onions, chopped
1 sprig fresh parsley
1 bay leaf
salt and freshly ground black pepper
1 1/2lb/750g uncooked prawns, shelled
  and deveined, leaving tail shells intact
Sauce Verte
3–4 spinach or chard leaves, stems
  removed
3/4 cup/175mL mayonnaise
3–4 tablespoons/45–60mL finely
  chopped fresh parsley
2 tablespoons/25mL snipped fresh chives

1 tablespoon/15mL finely chopped fresh
  dill or 1/2 teaspoon/2mL dried
For Garnish
8 small leaves mixed lettuce
chopped fresh parsley and slivered green
  onion greens or chives

METHOD

1. Place vermouth, green onions, parsley sprig and bay leaf in a saucepan, season to taste with salt and black pepper and bring to simmering. Add prawns and simmer gently for 2–3 minutes or until tender and pink. Drain and cool.

2. To make sauce, steam spinach or chard in a saucepan, covered, over moderate heat for 1 minute only. Cool quickly in cold water, drain and pat dry on paper towels. Finely chop. Place mayonnaise in a bowl, add spinach, parsley, chives and dill and mix to combine.

3. To serve, smear a little sauce in a semi-circle on four entrée plates. Arrange prawns on sauce, garnish with lettuce leaves and sprinkle with parsley and green onions or chives.

Serves 4

Prawns in Tomato Sauce

INGREDIENTS

1/4 cup/50mL butter
1 large onion (finely chopped)
1 clove garlic, crushed
4 large ripe tomatoes, skinned and chopped
1 tablespoon/15mL tomato paste
2 cups/500mL/16fl oz dry white wine
1 bay leaf
salt and pepper
2lb/1kg cooked prawns
6 shallots (chopped)

METHOD

1. Heat butter in pan, add onion and garlic. Cook until onion is soft.

2. Add tomatoes, tomato paste, wine and bay leaf, and season to taste with salt and pepper. Bring to boil, reduce heat, and simmer uncovered for 30 minutes or until sauce is reduced and thickened. Remove bay leaf.

3. Add shelled prawns and chopped shallots, and simmer gently until prawns are heated through.

Serves 4

Chili Prawn Pizza

INGREDIENTS

frozen pizza crust
tablespoons/45mL tomato paste (purée)
teaspoons/10mL vegetable oil
teaspoon/5mL ground cumin
fresh red chilies, seeded and chopped
cloves garlic, crushed
tablespoons/25mL lemon juice
lb/500g uncooked prawns,
shelled and deveined
red bell pepper, sliced
yellow or green bell pepper, sliced
tablespoons/25mL chopped cilantro
tablespoons/25mL grated Parmesan
cheese
reshly ground black pepper

METHOD

. Place pizza crust on a lightly greased
aking tray, spread with tomato paste and
et aside.

. Heat oil in a frying pan over a medium
eat, add cumin, chilies and garlic and cook,
tirring, for 1 minute.

. Stir in lemon juice and prawns and cook
r 3 minutes longer or until prawns just
hange color and are almost cooked.

. Top pizza base with red bell pepper, yellow
r green bell pepper, then with prawn mixture,
ilantro, Parmesan cheese and black pepper to
aste. Bake at 370°F/190°C for 20 minutes or
ntil base is crisp and golden.

Serves 4

93

Penne with Saffron and Prawns

INGREDIENTS

1lb/500g penne

<u>Saffron Sauce</u>

2 tablespoons/25mL butter

1 tablespoon/15ml all-purpose flour

1 cup/250mL/8fl oz 2% milk

**¹/₂ teaspoon/2mL saffron threads or
pinch saffron powder**

**1 tablespoon/15mL chopped fresh sage
or ¹/₂ teaspoon/2mL dried sage**

**1lb/500g cooked prawns, shelled
and deveined**

1 cup/250mL snow peas, blanched

METHOD

1. Cook pasta in boiling water in a large saucepan following package directions. Drain, set aside and keep warm.

2. To make sauce, melt butter in a small saucepan over a medium heat, stir in flour and cook for 1 minute. Remove pan from heat and whisk in milk, saffron and sage. Return pan to heat and cook, stirring, for 3–4 minutes or until sauce boils and thickens.

3. Add prawns and snow peas to hot pasta and toss to combine. Top with sauce and serve immediately.

Serves 4

Leek and Prawn Risotto

INGREDIENTS

1 tablespoon/15mL butter

4 leeks, sliced

**1 lb/500g medium uncooked prawns, shelled
and deveined**

2 cups/500mL arborio or risotto rice

**4 cups/1 litre/1³/₄ pt hot fish or vegetable
stock**

1 cup/250mL/8fl oz dry white wine

**1 tablespoon/15mL canned green
peppercorns, drained**

METHOD

1. Melt butter in a saucepan over a low heat, add leeks and cook, stirring occasionally, for 8 minutes or until leeks are soft, golden and caramelized. Add prawns and cook, stirring, for 3 minutes or until they just change color. Remove prawn mixture from pan and set aside.

2. Add rice to pan and cook over a medium heat, stirring, for 4 minutes. Stir in ³/₄ cup/175mL hot stock and ¹/₄ cup/50mL wine and cook, stirring constantly, over medium heat until liquid is absorbed. Continue adding stock and wine as described, stirring constantly and allowing stock to be absorbed before adding more.

3. Return prawn mixture to pan, add green peppercorns. Mix gently to combine and cook for 3 minutes longer or until heated through.

Serves 4

Penne with Saffron and Prawns

Spanish Carrot and Prawn Salad

INGREDIENTS

1½ lbs/700g carrots
4 cloves garlic
1 tablespoon/15mL fresh rosemary
¼ cup/50mL/2fl oz virgin olive oil
1 teaspoon/5mL ground cumin
2 teaspoons/10mL mild paprika
3 tablespoons/45mL white wine vinegar
salt and freshly ground pepper to taste
1 lb/500g large peeled, cooked prawns
   (tail on)
¼ bunch parsley, chopped

METHOD

1. Peel and trim the carrots, then slice on the diagonal into ¼in/5mm slices. Add the carrots to some salted boiling water and cook for 3–4 minutes or until almost crisp-tender, then drain.

2. Peel garlic and pound in a mortar and pestle with the fresh rosemary until ground.

3. Heat a teaspoon/5mL of oil in a small frypan and add the garlic and rosemary mixture, cumin and paprika and sauté for a minute or two. Remove from the heat and whisk in the remaining olive oil and white wine vinegar. Add salt and pepper to taste.

4. Toss the carrot slices and cooked prawns with the warm garlic rosemary dressing. Chill for at least 4 hours then serve cool or room temperature. Garnish with fresh parsley.

Serves 6

Pasta Shells with Prawn and Tomato Sauce

INGREDIENTS

3/4 cup/175mL olive oil
2 cloves garlic, halved
3 x 14oz/398mL cans peeled tomatoes,
   drained, seeded
2 tablespoons/25mL finely chopped parsley
salt
freshly ground black pepper
8oz/250g uncooked prawns, shelled,
   deveined and tails left intact
1lb/500g pasta shells

METHOD

1. Cook oil and garlic in a heavy-based saucepan over moderate heat until garlic is brown. Discard garlic.

2. Add tomatoes to hot oil. Simmer about 8 minutes, breaking up tomatoes with a wooden spoon. The sauce should stay lumpy. Add parsley, season to taste with salt and pepper.

3. Add prawns to tomato sauce, stir over heat until prawns change color. Keep warm.

4. Cook pasta shells in boiling salted water until al dente. Drain. Place in a heated bowl. Pour sauce over pasta shells, toss to coat well.

Serves 4

Prawns with Feta

INGREDIENTS

1 small onion, finely chopped
1 tablespoon/15mL butter
1 tablespoon/15mL olive oil
1/2 cup/125mL/4fl oz dry white wine
4 tomatoes, peeled, seeded and chopped
1 clove garlic, crushed
3/4 teaspoon/4mL chopped fresh oregano
salt
freshly ground black pepper
4oz/125g feta cheese, crumbled
2lb/1kg uncooked prawns, peeled and deveined
4 tablespoons/60mL chopped fresh parsley

METHOD

1. Sauté onion in butter and olive oil in a saucepan for 5 minutes. Add wine, tomatoes, garlic and oregano. Season with salt and pepper.

2. Bring to the boil, then simmer until sauce thickens slightly. Add cheese, mix well, then simmer for 10 minutes stirring occasionally.

3. Add prawns and cook over moderate heat for 5 minutes or until tender. Do not overcook. Transfer to a serving dish, sprinkle with parsley.

Serves 4

Prawns with Spinach

INGREDIENTS

^{1}/3 cup/100mL/3^1/2fl oz olive oil

1 onion, diced

1 red bell pepper, seeded and diced

1 clove garlic, crushed

2 tomatoes, peeled and diced

1 ^{1}/2 bunches spinach, washed and
  roughly chopped

2 tablespoons/25mL dry white wine

juice of 1 lemon

salt and freshly ground black pepper

1 lb/500g green prawns, shelled and
  deveined

lemon wedges (to garnish)

METHOD

1. Heat 2 tablespoons/25mL of the olive oil in
a saucepan and brown the onion. Add the red
pepper, garlic and tomatoes, and cook for
7 minutes. Add the spinach, white wine,
lemon juice and seasoning.

2. Cover and simmer gently for 8–10 minutes
(until the spinach is tender). Take off the heat.
Stir and keep warm.

3. Add the remaining oil to a large frying pan.
Once hot, add the prawns and sauté, stirring
constantly, for 3 minutes, or until just cooked.

4. Spoon the prawns into the spinach, fold to
combine, and spoon onto a warm serving platter
and garnish with lemon wedges.

Serves 4

Linguine with Prawns and Scallops in a Roasted Tomato Sauce

INGREDIENTS

14oz/400g linguine

2 lb/1kg tomatoes

olive oil (small quantity to drizzle over tomatoes)

salt and pepper

$1/3$ cup/85mL/3fl oz olive oil (in addition to above)

7oz/200g scallops

7oz/200g green prawns, peeled

$5^1/4$oz/150g calamari, cut into rings

7oz/200g firm white fish pieces

3 garlic cloves, crushed

2 onions, diced

1 tablespoon/15mL tomato paste (optional)

$1/3$ cup/85mL/3fl oz water

$1/2$ bunch parsley, chopped

Parmesan cheese

METHOD

1. Cook the linguine in salted boiling water until al dente and set aside.

2. To roast the tomatoes: preheat the oven to 350°F/180°C. Cut the tomatoes in half and place on a baking tray. Drizzle with olive oil, sprinkle with a little salt and pepper, and roast in the oven for 20–25 minutes.

3. Place in a food processor and process for a few seconds, but do not over-process. (The mixture should still have texture.)

4. Heat half the oil in a pan, and sauté the scallops and the prawns for 2 minutes until just cooked and remove from the pan. Add the calamari and cook for 2 minutes, before removing from the pan. Adding a little more oil if needed, sauté the fish for a few minutes until just cooked, and remove from the pan.

5. Heat the remaining oil, and sauté the garlic and onion for a few minutes until cooked. Add the tomato mixture, tomato paste if using, and water, and simmer for 10 minutes. Carefully add the seafood to the sauce, season with salt and pepper, and mix through the chopped parsley.

6. Serve with the linguine and Parmesan cheese.

Serves 4

...ine with Prawns and Scallops in a Roasted Tomato Sauce

Spanish Rice with Scampi and Prawns

Spanish Rice with Scampi and Prawns

INGREDIENTS

3 tablespoons/45mL olive oil

1 medium onion, finely chopped

2 fresh squid, cleaned and finely chopped

1 large ripe tomato, skinned and chopped

1¼ cups/300mL short-grain rice

3 cups/750mL/24fl oz water

pinch saffron threads

salt and ground pepper, to taste

8–16 fresh or thawed frozen scampi

1lb/500g fresh green king prawns

METHOD

1. In a large, heavy, flameproof deep frying pan heat the oil and gently fry the chopped onion and squid for about 5 minutes. Add the tomato and cook for a further 5 minutes.

2. Add rice and stir to mix well with the squid mixture for a minute or two. Bring water to boil with the saffron, salt and ground pepper and pour over the rice.

2. Add the shellfish, leaving the scampi either whole or halved and shelling the prawns or leaving them whole and unshelled.

3. Simmer over gentle heat until rice is cooked. The rice should not be stirred at all during the cooking so that the shellfish sits on top.

Serves 4

Spaghetti Marinara

INGREDIENTS

1 lb/500g spaghetti
2 teaspoons/10mL vegetable oil
2 teaspoons/10mL butter
2 onions, chopped
2 x 14oz/398mL canned tomatoes,
  undrained and mashed
2 tablespoons/25mL chopped fresh basil
  or 1 teaspoon/5mL dried basil
1/4 cup/50mL/2fl oz dry white wine
12 mussels, scrubbed and beards removed
12 scallops
12 uncooked prawns, shelled and deveined
4oz/125g calamari (squid) rings

METHOD

1. Cook pasta in boiling water in a large saucepan following package directions. Drain, set aside and keep warm.

2. Heat oil and butter in a frying pan over a medium heat. Add onions and cook, stirring, for 4 minutes or until onions are golden.

3. Stir in tomatoes, basil and wine, bring to simmering and simmer for 8 minutes. Add mussels, scallops and prawns and cook for 2 minutes longer.

4. Add calamari (squid) and cook for 1 minute or until shellfish is cooked. Spoon shellfish mixture over hot pasta and serve immediately.

Serves 4

Prawns with Garlic and Rosemary

INGREDIENTS

1 lb/500g green prawns, shelled and
  deveined
2 cloves garlic, crushed
3 tablespoons/45mL olive oil
1/4 teaspoon/1mL ground black pepper
2 sprigs fresh rosemary
3 tablespoons/45mL butter
1/2 cup/125mL/4fl oz dry vermouth

METHOD

1. In a large bowl, combine the prawns, garlic, olive oil, pepper and rosemary, tossing well. Cover and allow to marinate in the refrigerator for 8 hours or overnight.

2. In a large frying pan, melt the butter over high heat, add the prawns and marinade and sauté until pink, about 2 minutes.

3. Transfer prawns to a bowl with a slotted spoon. Discard rosemary sprigs. Pour the vermouth into the frying pan, bring to the boil and reduce to a moderately thick consistency.

4. Return prawns to the pan and toss in the glaze. Spoon prawns into serving dish and serve immediately.

Serves 4

Spaghetti Marinara

Prawns with Garlic and Rosemary

Spicy Prawns with Sun-Dried Tomatoes

INGREDIENTS

3 tablespoons/45mL olive oil
2 lb/1kg green king prawns, peeled, deveined, tails intact
1 tablespoon/15mL tomato paste
2 teaspoon2/10mL brown sugar
2 cloves garlic, crushed
1 tablespoon/15mL chili sauce
1 tablespoon/15mL cilantro, chopped
6^1/2oz/180g sun-dried tomatoes, drained
1 tablespoon/15mL fresh lime juice
snow pea sprouts, for garnish

METHOD

1. Heat the oil in a frying pan over moderate heat. Add the prawns and cook for 1 minute each side. Remove prawns with a slotted spoon and set aside.

2. Add the tomato paste, sugar, garlic, chili sauce and cilantro to frying pan and cook for 1 minute.

3. Return prawns to frying pan, add sun-dried tomatoes, toss in chili sauce and sprinkle with lime juice. Place prawns on a serving plate.

4. Garnish with snow pea sprouts and serve.

Serves 4

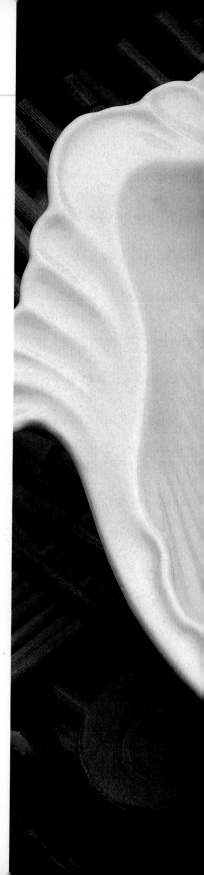

Pasta with Lobster and Prawns

INGREDIENTS

1 lb/500g small pasta shells
8oz/250g cooked prawns, shelled
lemon juice for prawns and lobster
1 cooked lobster
1 onion, chopped
2 cloves garlic, crushed
butter
1 cup/250g/8oz fresh tomato purée
1 tablespoon/15mL tomato paste
$^{1}/_{2}$ cup/125mL/4fl oz white wine
$^{3}/_{4}$ cup/175mL/6fl oz cream
parsley

METHOD

1. Cook pasta in rapidly boiling salted water until al dente. Keep warm.

2. Sprinkle shelled prawns with lemon juice and chill. After cleaning and shelling lobster, slice into rounds, sprinkle with lemon juice.

3. Take a frying pan and cook the onion and garlic in butter. Combine tomato purée and paste with wine and add to onion mixture.

4. Simmer and when sauce is thickened, add cream, stirring well. Add seafood to the hot sauce. When thoroughly heated serve with cooked pasta. Garnish with parsley.

Serves 6

FAVORITE
PRAWNS

Our last section is a selection of prawn dishes we know you will enjoy. Such favorites as Prawn Tacos, Prawn and Pineapple Curry and Prawns with Garlic and Wine Sauce are always enjoyed, often with requests for seconds.

Butterflied Prawns with Garlic, Chili & Parsley

INGREDIENTS

2 lb/1kg (approx. 20) green prawns,
  shelled, deveined, tails intact
2 tablespoons/25mL olive oil
1 tablespoon/15mL lemon juice
2 cloves garlic, crushed
2 red chilies, seeded and finely chopped
2 tablespoons/25mL parsley, chopped
1/2 cup/125mL flour
all-purpose flour (for coating prawns)
oil (for frying)
lemon wedges and parsley (to garnish)

METHOD

1. Cut prawns down the back and remove vein.

2. Combine oil, lemon juice, garlic, chili and parsley in a bowl. Add prawns, mix well, and leave to marinate for 2–3 hours.

3. Heat oil in a large pan, coat prawns with flour, and cook quickly in oil for 2–3 minutes. Drain on absorbent paper towels.

4. Serve with lemon wedges and parsley.

Serves 6

Potted Prawns

INGREDIENTS

1/2 cup/175mL butter
1lb/500g uncooked peeled prawns, cut
  into small pieces
1/2 teaspoon/2mL ground mixed spice
1/2 teaspoon/2mL each freshly grated
  mace and nutmeg
pinch cayenne pepper
freshly ground black pepper
hot toast triangles or melba toast to
  serve

METHOD

1. Melt butter in a frying pan over moderate heat until foaming subsides. Add prawns and spices, seasoning to taste, and cook, stirring, for 2–3 minutes or until prawns are pink and cooked.

2. Spoon mixture into four individual serving pots, pressing lightly. Cover prawns with rounds of aluminium foil then with a lid or extra foil and refrigerate for 2–3 hours or until firm. Serve with toast.

Serves 4

Butterflied Prawns with Garlic, Chili & Parsley

Prawn Jambalaya

INGREDIENTS

3 strips bacon, cut into pieces
1 large onion, finely chopped
1 green pepper, diced
1 stalk celery, chopped
3 cloves garlic, crushed
1 cup/250mL long-grain rice
1^1/2–3 cups/375–500mL boiling
chicken stock
14oz/398mL can tomatoes, drained
and mashed
2 teaspoons/10mL Cajun spice mix
1 teaspoon/5mL dried thyme
1lb/500g uncooked medium prawns, shelled
and deveined
5^1/2oz/155g smoked ham in one piece, cut
into ^{1}/2in/1cm cubes
3 green onions, finely chopped

METHOD

1. Cook bacon in a frying pan over a medium heat for 5 minutes or until crisp. Remove bacon from pan and drain on paper towels.

2. Add onion to pan and cook, stirring, for 5 minutes or until onion is soft, but not brown. Add green pepper, celery and garlic and cook for 3 minutes. Add rice and cook, stirring frequently, for 5 minutes or until rice becomes translucent.

3. Stir in stock, tomatoes, spice mix and thyme and bring to the boil. Cover, reduce heat to low and cook for 15 minutes. Stir in prawns, bacon and ham, cover and cook for 10 minutes longer or until rice is tender and liquid absorbed. Sprinkle with green onions and serve immediately.

Serves 4

FAVORITES

6

Prawn Tostaditas

INGREDIENTS

Prawn and Vegetable Topping

1 cob sweet corn
1 red bell pepper, quartered
1 yellow bell pepper, quartered
2 teaspoons/10mL vegetable oil
1 red onion, cut into wedges
13^1/$_4$oz/375g medium uncooked prawns,
  shelled and deveined
4 mild fresh green chilies, cut
  into strips
1 tablespoon/15mL lime juice
vegetable oil (for frying tortillas)
8 corn tortillas
^{1}/$_2$ avocado, chopped
2 tablespoons/25mL chopped fresh mint

METHOD

1. To make topping, place sweet corn cob and red and yellow bell peppers on a preheated hot barbecue or grill and cook until lightly charred. Cut corn from cob and set aside. Cut peppers into strips and set aside.

2. Heat 2 teaspoons/10mL of oil in a frying pan over a medium heat, add onion and cook for 4 minutes or until golden. Add prawns, chilies and lime juice and cook for 2 minutes or until prawns change color. Add sweet corn kernels and red and yellow peppers, toss to combine and set aside.

3. Heat 1 in/2^1/$_2$cm oil in a frying pan over a medium heat until a cube of bread dropped in browns in 50 seconds. Cook tortillas, one at time, for 45 seconds each side or until crisp. Drain on paper towels.

4. To serve, pile topping onto tortillas, then scatter with avocado and mint. Serve immediately.

Serves 4

Shrimp Creole

Yucateco Seafood Risotto

INGREDIENTS

1 lb/500g assorted seafood such as
  prawns, calamari and scallops
1 lb/500g white fish fillets (no bones)
2 tablespoons/25mL olive oil
$^1/_4$-$^1/_2$ teaspoon/1–2mL minced chili
2 cloves garlic, crushed
1 tablespoon/15mL olive oil
2 onions, sliced
1$^3/_4$ cup/425mL arborio rice
1 cup/250mL/8fl oz white wine
2 bay leaves
2 potatoes, peeled and diced
2 stalks celery, sliced
3 cups/750mL rich fish stock,
  simmering
2 large tomatoes, chopped
$^1/_2$ cup/125mL milk or hot taco
  sauce
$^1/_3$ cup/100mL cream
1 bunch parsley, chopped
2 potatoes, boiled and thinly sliced
1 teaspoon/5mL paprika

METHOD

1. Prepare and rinse the shellfish. Cut the fish fillets into 1in/2$^1/_2$cm chunks. Heat the olive oil and sauté the chili, garlic and fish chunks until opaque. Remove with a slotted spoon and keep warm. Add the shellfish to the same pan and sauté until just cooked and changed color, about 3 minutes. Remove the pan from the heat, return the fish and mix gently. Set aside.

INGREDIENTS

$^1/_4$ cup/50mL/2fl oz olive oil
2 lb/1kg green prawns, shelled
1 large onion, finely chopped
1 green bell pepper
1 large stalk celery
4 large ripe tomatoes, peeled and chopped
2 cups/500mL/16fl oz fish stock (or stock
  made from prawn heads and shells)
salt and freshly ground pepper
pinch cayenne
bouquet garni
chopped parsley

METHOD

1. Heat oil in large heavy frypan and sauté prawns, onion, green bell pepper and celery for a few minutes until softened. Add chopped tomatoes, fish stock, salt, pepper, cayenne and bouquet garni. Bring to simmer and cook for about 25 minutes.

2. Scoop away the vegetables and set aside, leaving the liquid in the pan. Reduce the liquid over a moderate heat to about half, then return vegetables along with the prawns.

3. Simmer for 5 minutes, remove bouquet garni and serve sprinkled with parsley.

Serves 4

2. In a large saucepan, heat the olive oil and sauté the onions. Add the rice and stir to coat, allowing the rice to become translucent. Add the wine and allow to simmer until the liquid evaporates. Add the bay leaves, potato cubes and celery with the first addition of half a cup/125mL of stock. Stir vigorously to combine. When the stock has been absorbed, add the next half cup/125mL of stock. Continue in this fashion, adding stock and stirring thoroughly until the last quantity of stock is to be added.

3. At this time, add the chopped tomatoes, milk or taco sauce, cream and half the parsley. When all the ingredients have been added and most of the stock has been absorbed, remove the pan from the heat, remove the bay leaves and serve in individual bowls on a bed of boiled sliced potatoes, garnished with plenty of parsley and a sprinkling of paprika.

Serves 6

Yucateco Seafood Risotto

Seafood with Green Vegetables

6

Seafood with Green Vegetables

INGREDIENTS

1 cup/250mL snow peas
1 cup/250mL broccoli, broken into small
  florets
8–10 asparagus spears, trimmed
1½ cups/375mL fish stock
8oz/225g large uncooked prawns, shelled
  and deveined, tails intact
8oz/225g firm white fish fillets, cut into
  ¾in/2 cm cubes
8oz/225g scallops
½ cup/125mL/4fl oz heavy or whipping
  cream
¼ cup/50mL/2fl oz tomato purée
1 tablespoon/15mL chopped fresh tarragon
  or 1 teaspoon/5mL dried tarragon
freshly ground black pepper

METHOD

1. Steam or microwave snow peas, broccoli and asparagus, separately, until just tender. Drain, refresh under cold running water and set aside.

2. Place stock in a large saucepan and bring to the boil, add prawns, fish and scallops to stock and cook for 5 minutes or until just cooked. Using a slotted spoon, remove and set aside.

3. Stir in cream, tomato purée and tarragon and bring to the boil. Reduce heat and simmer for 10 minutes or until liquid is reduced by one-third. Add reserved vegetables and seafood to sauce and cook for 1–2 minutes or until heated through. Season to taste with black pepper and serve immediately.

Serves 4

Prawns in Peppercorn Sauce

INGREDIENTS

3 tablespoons/45mL butter
5 tablespoons/75mL all-purpose flour
2 cups/500mL/16fl oz milk
1 cup/250mL/8fl oz chicken stock
pinch ground cayenne pepper
½ teaspoon/2mL dry mustard
2 tablespoons/25mL sherry
½ cup/125mL/4fl oz cream
1 tablespoon/15mL canned green
  peppercorns (rinsed)
4 lb/2kg cooked medium king prawns
  (peeled and deveined)

METHOD

1. Heat butter in a large saucepan, stir in flour, and cook (stirring) for 2 minutes.

2. Over low heat, gradually stir in milk and stock, cook (stirring continuously) until mixture thickens and boils.

3. Add cayenne, mustard, sherry, cream, peppercorns and prawns. Simmer gently until prawns are heated through.

Serves 6

Almond Crumbed Prawns

INGREDIENTS

1½ lb/750g green king prawns
½ cup/125mL all-purpose flour
1 egg
⅓ cup/75mL milk
1¾ cups/425mL almonds (blanched and
  finely chopped)
oil (for deep frying)

METHOD

1. Shell prawns (leaving tails intact, but remove vein). Cut prawns down back, and spread out flat.

2. Sift flour into bowl, make a well in the center, add combined beaten egg and milk, and gradually stir in flour. Beat until smooth.

3. Dip prawns into batter, and then roll in finely chopped almonds.

4. Drop into hot oil, and fry until golden brown.

Serves 4–6

Prawn and Pineapple Curry

INGREDIENTS

1 stalk lemongrass, roughly chopped
5 green onions, peeled
3 cloves garlic, peeled
4 fresh red chilies, halved and seeded
1 teaspoon/5mL ground turmeric
3 tablespoons/45mL chopped cilantro
6 tablespoons/90mL vegetable oil
1/2 teaspoon/2mL shrimp paste
1 can coconut milk
1lb/500g green king prawns,
** shelled and deveined**
1 can sliced pineapple
salt, to taste

METHOD

1. Using a blender or food processor grind the lemongrass with the green onions, garlic, chilies, turmeric and cilantro.

2. Heat the oil in a wok and add the ground paste. Cook for a minute then stir in shrimp paste with the thin part of the coconut milk. When mixture is bubbling stir in the prawns and the remaining coconut milk.

3. Allow to heat for a few minutes then stir in drained, sliced pineapple pieces and continue to simmer for about 10 minutes. Season to taste. Serve with steamed rice.

Serves 4

Baked Mushrooms
Stuffed with Prawns

INGREDIENTS

4 tablespoons/60mL vegetable oil
1 small carrot, cut into julienne strips
1 stalk celery, cut into julienne strips
$^1/_2$ leek or onion, cut into julienne strips
8 large mushrooms, stems removed
$^1/_2$ cup/125mL butter
1lb/500g green prawns, shelled and
  deveined, tails intact
4 cloves garlic, crushed
4 tablespoons/60mL chopped fresh
  parsley
3 tablespoons/45mL fresh lemon juice
salt
freshly ground black pepper

METHOD

1. Heat oil in a frying pan over moderate heat and cook carrot, celery and leek or onion, stirring, until cooked but still crisp. Using a slotted spoon, remove vegetables to a plate. Add mushrooms to pan and cook, stirring, for 1 minute each side. Arrange mushrooms in a baking dish. Preheat oven to 350°F/180°C.

2. Melt butter in frying pan over moderate heat until foaming subsides, add prawns and garlic and cook, stirring, until pink and cooked. Add parsley and lemon juice to pan, season to taste with salt and black pepper and heat through, stirring. Remove pan from heat. Reserve a few prawns for garnish.

3. Cut remaining prawns into small pieces, arrange in mushroom caps and bake for 4–6 minutes or until heated through and bubbly. Return vegetables to frying pan, season to taste with salt and black pepper and heat through.

4. To serve, arrange 2 mushrooms on each heated entrée plate, spoon vegetables onto plates, garnish with reserved prawns and serve immediately.

This robust dish is well-flavored with garlic.

Serves 4

Mexican Prawns with Salsa

INGREDIENTS

1¹/₂lb/750g uncooked large prawns,
   shelled and deveined
2 tablespoons/25mL lime juice
2 teaspoons/10mL ground cumin
2 tablespoons/25mL chopped fresh cilantro
2 fresh red chilies, chopped
2 teaspoons/10mL vegetable oil
<u>Avocado Salsa</u>
1 avocado, pitted, peeled and chopped
1 tablespoon/15mL lemon juice
¹/₂ red bell pepper, chopped
2 green onions, chopped
¹/₂ teaspoon/2mL chili powder
1 tablespoon fresh cilantro

4 tortillas or flat bread

METHOD

1. Place prawns, lime juice, cumin, chopped cilantro, chilies and oil in a bowl, toss to combine and set aside to marinate for 5 minutes.

2. To make salsa, place avocado, lemon juice, red bell pepper, green onions, chili powder and cilantro in a bowl and mix gently to combine. Set aside.

3. Heat a nonstick frying pan over a high heat, add prawns and stir-fry for 4–5 minutes or until prawns are cooked. To serve, divide prawns among tortillas or flat bread and top with salsa.

Serves 4

Prawn Ceviche

INGREDIENTS

1lb/500g medium green prawns, shelled
   and deveined
³/₄ cup/175mL/6fl oz lime juice
³/₄ cup/175mL/6fl oz lemon juice
¹/₂ cup/125mL/4fl oz orange juice
1 fresh hot chili, cut into strips
1 clove garlic, crushed
1 teaspoon/5mL brown sugar
1 red bell pepper, cut into strips
¹/₂ small red onion, cut into strips
2 tablespoons/25mL chopped cilantro
2 ripe tomatoes, seeded and diced
salt and ground black pepper

METHOD

1. In a bowl, marinate prawns in a mixture of the citrus juices, chili, garlic and sugar for at least 6 hours or overnight. This marinade will "cold cook" the prawns. The prawns should lose their translucent appearance.

2. Remove prawns from marinade and toss with remaining ingredients, seasoning well with salt and freshly ground black pepper.

Serves 4 as an appetizer

Mexican Prawns with Salsa

Prawn Ceviche

King Prawns in a Sweet Potato Crust

INGREDIENTS

Prawns

1 lb/500g large raw prawns, peeled and deveined

2 green onions, finely chopped

1 stalk lemongrass, finely chopped

1 tablespoon/15mL fresh ginger, minced

1/2 bunch cilantro, finely chopped

1 teaspoon/5mL fish sauce

1 tablespoon/15mL sweet chili sauce

Batter

1 large or 2 small sweet potatoes

1/2 teaspoon/2mL turmeric

1 cup/250mL/8fl oz coconut milk

1/2 cup/125mL/4fl oz water

1/2 cup/125mL self-rising flour

1/2 cup/125mL rice flour

1 tablespoon/15mL polenta

2 tablespoons/25mL peanut oil

lime wedges for serving

METHOD

1. Chop the prawns roughly and mix with the finely chopped green onions, lemongrass, fresh ginger, cilantro, fish sauce and sweet chili sauce. Marinate for 1 hour.

2. Meanwhile, grate the sweet potato. In a separate bowl, mix the turmeric, coconut milk, water, self-rising flour, rice flour and polenta. Stir thoroughly to combine, then add the grated sweet potato and set aside until prawns are ready. Combine the prawn mixture with the batter and mix thoroughly.

3. Heat a non-stick frypan with peanut oil and drop spoonfuls of the prawn mixture into the frypan. Cook over a medium-high heat for three minutes on each side, or until the underside is crisp and golden. Turn them over and cook the other side.

4. When cooked, remove the fritters from the frypan. Allow them to cool on a wire rack, or serve immediately with lime wedges.

To reheat, place the wire rack in the oven (preheated to 400°F/200°C) for 5–10 minutes.

Variation: If you do not wish to use shellfish, substitute fresh salmon for the prawns and dice before mixing with the marinade ingredients. Then proceed with the recipe above. A combination of prawns and salmon also works very well.

Makes 12–16 fritters

INDEX

INDEX